Anne McKevitt's
house
sensation

Anne McKevitt's
house
sensation

brilliant and
imaginative ideas
for transforming
your **home**

special photography by **Colin Poole**

Quadrille

dedications

This book is dedicated to the memory of Linda McCartney, without whose help and intervention after my car accident, I may never have lived and walked properly again. She was a very special lady with a big heart, who should be remembered for her tireless campaigning for animal rights and vegetarianism. As Linda said: 'Don't eat anything that has a face.'

To Don for putting up with me through highs and lows. You've always been wonderful.
To my Mum Jenny for always expecting things to happen.

publishing director: **anne furniss**
art director: **mary evans**
project editor: **pauline savage**
designers: **simon balley and joanna hill**
text editor: **hilary mandleberg**
technical editor: **mike lawrence**
illustrator: **james neal**
picture research: **nadine bazar**
production: **vincent smith, candida jackson**
special photography art direction and styling: **anne mckevitt**

First published in 1998 by Quadrille Publishing Ltd, Alhambra House,
27–31 Charing Cross Road, London WC2H 0LS

Cataloguing in Publication Data: a catalogue record for this book is available from the British Library.

ISBN 1 899988 43 2

Printed and bound by Arnoldo Mondadori Editore spa, Verona, Italy

contents

lifestyles

Lifestyle is a word that we see everywhere, the buzzword of the decade. With the everyday intrusion of the mass media into your home - newspapers, magazines, TV and films - examples of the current trends are available 24 hours a day, whether you want them or not. Through endless glossy pictures, we're encouraged to aspire to impractical designs and hopelessly unaffordable furnishings. It would seem that lifestyle is no longer a way of life, more a marketing concept.

For example, how many times do we read in books and magazines: 'This design would suit an impromptu dinner party'? Well, not in my house, that's for sure! But just because I don't rustle up a three-course meal every evening, doesn't mean that there's no point in my contemplating a dining area. After all, food doesn't have to be the main focus. Today's eating areas should be observation points, enlivening if you are on your own or encapsulating if you are part of a group.

The kind of home you have and the mood, ambience and style of decor you create, should be perfectly designed to suit your lifestyle. What people want are real homes, not some prissy designer showcase that looks like a stage set. Similarly, deciding on a style for old houses should be determined by the lifestyle

below: **A magnificent living room with beautiful proportions of light and space is overlooked by an immense gallery. The central fireplace with its tall flue is the jewel in the crown.**

you choose and not by the tired traditions of a bygone era. After two decades of paint effects, heritage nostalgia and tassle hassles, now is the time to go back to your roots. And this is what this book is all about: helping you to decide what you want from your home, inspiring you to achieve it, and abandoning convention whenever possible along the way.

Five elements run throughout this book: Light, Space, Colour, Texture and Detail. Each room featured in the book focuses in some way on one of these elements. Transforming your home with them in mind helps to break down what can often seem a mammoth task and to focus on the basics. But first, you need to contemplate how you really live.

Rather than having a rose-tinted view of your normal day, be realistic. This will help you evaluate the importance of everything around you. One of the best ways of doing this is to clear all your furniture and possessions from the room in question and paint the walls in a neutral shade like cream. Living in it like this for a couple of weeks can be a very liberating experience. You will find that the essentials soon creep back into the room, while all those things you've simply got used to having around but which never feature in your daily existence do not. If you can't be this disciplined, try to spend half an hour analysing your existing room layout on three occasions over a two-week period. Once you've edited the so-called essentials down to a bare minimum, you can start to detox your home and use space efficiently.

top: **An acid-yellow capsule kitchen commands a light and airy room where each piece of furniture is an object of desire.**

above: **Galvanized metal bath and walls contrast with the opaque shower curtain whose design reflects the shape of the window panes.**

above: **The uses of glass in design are as unbounded as your imagination. Here a flowing luminous strip of glass has been inserted into the concrete floor. Its simplicity of line and form make it all the more breathtaking.**

above right: **Think Manhattan. The hallway of a contemporary home has a sandwich of shelves between a wall of glass bricks and a metal staircase, creating a slim vertical library that is a feast for both the mind and eyes.**

The flow of your living space is vital for a harmonious existence. Start by reassessing the relationship between all the adjoining rooms. Is your eating area a long trek from the kitchen, so that by the time you've settled down to your food, it's stone cold? Does the position of your bathroom entail a chilly, dripping dash to somewhere warm where you can dress? Relocating the rooms in your home to suit your requirements is costly but by no means impossible.

Not surprisingly, people are often too nervous to undertake a large-scale transformation, opting instead for a cosmetic makeover. Wherever you are in the courage stakes, create a room that's really worth spending time in.

No room will ever look great without proper consideration of the light. There are several key lighting sources: natural light; task lighting (such as a reading light); ambient lighting (which casts few shadows and can be used to create mood); accent lighting (emphasizing a feature such as a painting or ornament); and decorative lighting (an attention-seeking embellishment).

But however much importance you give it, artificial lighting will never replace the glory of natural light. Subtle and never static, natural light should never be taken for granted. Surprisingly, many people fail to harness its potential, dressing windows in a way that blocks it out and undermines its power. Without even the flick of a switch that electricity requires, daylight can provide essential contrasts and diversity in a room. Diffused light and dappled patterns will dance around a living space. Left unfettered, natural light will warm up a room or throw deep shadows, depending on the time of day or year.

Colour is the most potent tool in decoration today. Available in various forms – paint, fabric, tiles, wallpaper and flooring – colour can change your life. I've always adored it, although I don't subscribe to a particular colour theory. I find that it's easier to follow what looks good to you. Colour goes hand in hand with light in creating the right feel for a room, but it is often the element people are most

left: **An understated bedroom with home office annexe has been decorated in subdued tones and textures. The bed is covered in an elegant iridescent fabric with just enough sheen to catch the light, while vast quantities of fabric partition the walls.**

conservative about. Natural colours - grey- or brown-based shades - have a pleasurable simplicity, and if you are a nervous decorator, naturals are a good starting point. They can be used to create calming, restful moods to which you can add details and accessories in contrasting accent colours. For example, if you adore a strong colour like purple but painting a room in it strikes fear into you, then pick up the purple in a couple of cushions, a throw or a vase.

Sight may be our dominant sense, but a home shouldn't just look great, it should feel fabulous as well. Humans need the physical touch. But it is the juxtaposition of contrasting textures that is really stimulating. So liberate your interior from smooth paintwork and flawless walls. Place an opulent duchess satin throw next to a cool concrete coffee table, apply exterior wall surfaces to your rooms.

Link rough with smooth, grainy with glossy, and learn how to invigorate and arouse your home.

But don't forget the detail - the finishing touches that can make or break a room. These need careful thought - the vases, lamps, cushions and pictures for a living area, the cutlery and glassware for eating, the sanitary ware for your bathroom, the linen for your bedroom. They need to be chosen so that they enhance rather than clash with your overall plan. But despite the range of wonderful designs available for these details, no man-made feature can ever replicate nature: evolution kindly gives an ever-changing feast

above: **Barns often bring out a sickly sentimental streak in people when they are renovating them. City slickers try to parody country life as they imagine it. Thankfully this barn conversion capitalizes on the building's space and structure to create a great design for modern living.**

for the eye. There is nothing more captivating than the simple beauty of organic shapes: the iridescent glaze of a shell, the running ripples of sand, bees' honeycomb. So bring as much of the outdoors into your home as possible.

Whether you are a new home-owner without much money to lavish on decor, or living in a rented property which has restrictions on what you can modify, or are about to launch into a major restructuring of your home, you'll find inspiration and encouragement in this book to express what you admire and install what you crave. Your home needs to reflect you, not the other way around. It's obvious - a better home means a better life. So dare to turn the mundane into the magnificent.

below left: **White walls are challenged as colour boldly moves into a contemporary living space. Individual sofas of aubergine and soft apple green are framed by an indigo-blue backdrop.**

below: **Exterior meets interior, with glass being the only divider between outdoor eating on the open-air terrace and indoor eating in the dining room.**

style and content

living

Save your home from the **enemy** of

humankind: a **nostalgic** longing for

tradition and heritage. Instead, **awaken**

your living space, redefine your

life and live in the world of today, where a

liberated modern home

means that **anything is**

possible...

tribal
instinct

I'm often asked how I create the whole look of a room. Every room is different. In the case of my own living room, I was drawn back to my childhood in Scotland, which gave me a deep appreciation of everything that nature has to offer. The taste for a hint of rugged northern Scotland coastline has stayed with me. I was also influenced by a book of tribal portrait photography that strengthened my belief in the centuries-old need in humans for self-adornment and decoration.

The images and influences in my living room are of a more primitive way of life, but adapted to enhance a sense of calm living in a twenty-first century room. In other words, my aim was to forge a link between our organic roots and the manufactured.

below left: **Cream carpet was fitted throughout the ground floor, but it was personalized by cutting in a river of blue, running from the front door directly through to the kitchen** (see page 161).

below right:
With the help of a structural engineer, change poky self-contained rooms into an obstacle-free living space (see page 149).

left: **Even the studded mirror** (see page 172) **is influenced by the skin scarification of the Bumi tribe of Ethiopia.**

below: **Pictures from a book of tribal portrait photography were cut out and framed to make this colourful gallery** (see page 174). **The diverse and vivid decoration of the faces became an inspiration for the whole room.**

space light colour texture detail

below: **Large spaces still need focal points. This simple fireplace and hearth replaced the replica turn-of-the-century version and can be made quite easily** (see page 180). See also page 164 for how to paint up and over colour.

above: **A 'revolutionary' idea for TV storage – and simple to create** (see page 154). **This revolving unit decorated with faces inspired by my tribal portraits allows the TV to be hidden away when not in use.**

left: **The buff willow screens give a change in wall texture and are reminiscent of African huts.**

organic

My living room was once four separate rooms: living and dining rooms, tiny annexe kitchen and hallway. Since I believe that architecture today should accommodate rather than dictate the way we live, one freeform space was more appealing, so I knocked the walls through.

The colour blocks on the walls were an exaggeration of the sooty charcoal and shocking red vegetable-dye-painted faces of my book of tribal portrait photography. Luscious chocolate brown contrasts with Icelandic blues combined with cobalt, indigo and crimson.

nuggets + no-nos

● **Think big: new furniture has to match the large scale of an open-plan room.**

● **Buying an old house doesn't mean you have to stick with its period features. Don't be afraid to mix traditional and modern.**

above: **An abstract light makes an unusual ceiling decoration** (see page 170).

The abstract, stand-alone sculptural elements in the room are statements that remind me of the rocky outcrops and coastline of my native Scotland. The most prominent of these are the dining table with its polished stones sandwiched between two layers of glass and the freestanding sculpture next to it. The two are the same shape - one lies horizontally, the other stands vertically. For more shape and texture but on a smaller scale, I also included cast-concrete pots and

lava-stone urns. To complement it all, I used classic
modern furniture in graphic shapes upholstered in
fabrics in a mixture of neutral shades and plucky
colours.

Finally, an ordinary door-
fronted bookcase provides
storage. Its rather bland
exterior was turned into
a stunning piece of
furniture by staining
each door with a
different wood dye.

tear down the walls and play with the space as you please

First impressions count, so turn your hallway and stairs into a prima donna. The entrance to your home is the artery to every other room, not just somewhere you pass through, so make it a place to behold. Adorn it with colour taken from the rest of your house, transforming it into an introduction to your home. Or, if you want a complete contrast, do what you'd be scared to attempt in an everyday room. As floor space is likely to be scarce, treat the walls as a surface to play with, your very own art gallery, and choose furniture that is brazen, confident and poised for comment. Lastly, remember to have somewhere to fling down your keys when you get home, so you can find them easily when you're rushing out again.

halls and staircases

right: **My staircase has gone through many transformations, but this is my favourite. The sculpted fretwork panel** (see page 173) **adds a personal touch, while the colour blocking in contrasting shades makes a bold statement and enlivens the walls.** See page 164 for how to paint up and over colour.

left and below: **Painted staircase treads open up a labyrinth of decorative possibilities which are all achievable on a tight budget. Here, the pressed leaf prints hanging on the wall are the inspiration for a vibrantly painted coloured runner** (see page 167).

right: **The branch console table** (see page 178), **made from fallen branches and plywood, brings nature right into your home. As well as a place for displaying items, it acts as camouflage for the radiator behind, allowing hot air to flow freely. The abstract mirror** (see page 172) **is perfectly placed for reflecting light back into the hallway.**

three lads
rent a pad

above: **If you can't put colour on your walls, why not do the next best thing and paint large canvases to look like abstract art** (see page 173)?

When three lads rent a pad together, it usually looks like the aftermath of a riot squad party - and that's on a good day! Obviously, not everyone in rented accommodation lives like this, but this nightmare scenario was true in the case of the three guys who shared this living room. But when I asked them how they would like the room to look, believe it or not they replied, 'like a New York loft apartment, quite minimalist'. In your dreams, guys!

With rented properties, there are often many restrictions on what you are allowed to do. In this case, the walls had to remain white, all the furniture had to stay and no solid partitions could be built. Of the existing furniture, only two sofas and a computer table were worth keeping. All the other objects were condemned to the understairs cupboard.

Fortunately, the landlord gave permission to throw out the dreadful carpet. Frustratingly, the floorboards did not match: all the replacement boards were a completely different variety and colour of wood.

right: **If you find your floorboards don't match, it's not the end of the world, as you can stain the odd ones out to match the rest** (see page 159).

inset: **A door wrapped in zinc and placed on trellis legs makes an unusual dining table. With the addition of a net, it can then double as a ping-pong table on nights when an à la carte menu isn't planned.**

space light colour texture detail

5 steps to a fab rented pad

❶ A quick coat of paint – even if it is a boring, landlord-specified colour – can do wonders for freshening up a tired, fading room.

❷ For the sake of your sanity, remove any bad-taste objects and store them away in a cupboard.

❸ Cover all stain-covered sofas and armchairs with inexpensive throws or bedspreads. Then, at least, you can sit down.

❹ Get pally with the landlord. Ask if they'd like the floorboards exposed and varnished an inviting honey yellow instead of covered with a gross carpet.

❺ There's no point spending money on things you'll have to leave behind: removable fabric runners and wall hangings change the space and mask unsightly objects.

However, you can get around this problem by staining the odd ones to match the originals – time-consuming, but better than painting the floor in a solid colour.

With a room that's techno-crazy you have two options – show it or stow it. With three guys sharing this room, it was obvious that the 'stow it' option was the only one worth considering. The room contained an alcove that was badly utilized. Some shelving and electrical outlets were installed, so that it could house the entire home entertainment mecca. All that was required was some groovy doors for it to be an inventive focal point for the room. The cut-out shapes not only looked funky but allowed access to some of the equipment when the doors were closed.

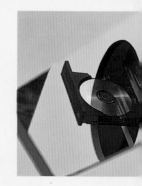

right: **Primary yellow doors provide the perfect hideaway for unsightly wiring and techno equipment.** See page 157 for how to make cool hi-fi storage.

skate off!

left: **Stumbling around after a heavy Saturday night could be fun with a skateboard coffee table about** (see page 178)! **With butch industrial castors to aid mobility, it is also a great stow-away space-saver.**

if you can't **bump off** your **landlord** there is **hope!**

left: **The window dressing is simple and easy to care for. The bottom half is covered with filmy green chiffon fabric, which has a series of buttonholes so that it can be attached to the bulky chrome doorknobs on the frame. Rattan blinds fixed to the top can be pulled down in the evenings.**

No lad's manhood is intact without his bike. By stringing this particular one up on a hoist directly in front of one of the canvases, it not only becomes a 'bit arty' - as requested by the boys - but is also kept out of the way.

A separate computer workzone was created at the far end of the room. A screening system, made from very inexpensive material attached to wire cables overhead, allowed the area to be shut away in the evenings.

The overhead lighting in the room consisted of three spotlights - not really the most attractive things to look at in a living room. A good way of disguising unsightly fittings like these is hang up a long piece

below left and right: **The movable screen is another great source of colour in the room and is a brilliant way to divide up the space without using a permanent structure.** See page 182 for how to make a fabric screen.

of billowing fabric, which also diffuses the
light. Ballooning fabric proved ideal: not
only flame retardant, but also
surprisingly inexpensive.

With a couple of colourful rugs, a
few plants and large bedspreads used
as sofa throws, a potential disaster
zone soon became a room well worth
living in.

● **Don't be put off a low-rent flat just because it's grungy. For the cost of two weeks' rent most places can be smartened up quite easily.**

● **You can also cheer up colourless walls by stapling fabric to them – but touch up hairpin holes afterwards.**

below left: **Fabric is an easy way to change the quality of light from harsh spotlight to soft and diffuse.** See page 170 for how to make a billowing light cover.

below right: **The bike used to get shoved, unloved, into a corner, until it was rescued and given pride of place, thanks to a handy cycle pulley system.**

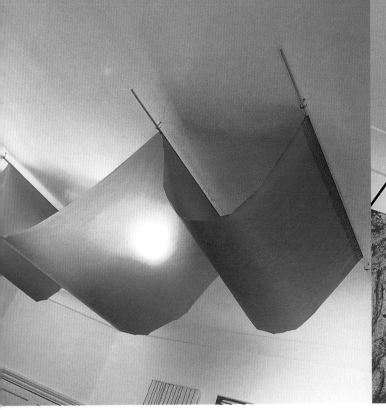

techno storage

High-tech home entertainment is paradise for the couch potato. Now techno items are no longer perceived just as pieces of electronic wizardry, but more as items of furniture with a personality all of their own. For some of us, the wraparound sound system and mammoth TV screen have become the most dominant features of the main room – a kind of New-Age altar. However, others go to great lengths in the concealment stakes, metamorphosing the beast in the corner into things like crass, unsightly fake drinks cabinets. If you are the sort of person who prefers concealment, then I recommend getting a custom-made piece of furniture to cage the beast in, or a screen of some sort to hide it from view. But if you are the exhibitionist type, pick components with impact and hope that they look good.

above: **This whimsical method of storing the TV proves that you don't need to rush out and buy the latest flatpack unit, when you can head to the garden centre and get a couple of trolley-loads of sandbags instead!**

left: **Great style is an elusive quality, very easy to recognize but often difficult to define. It is often about understatement. Here, an unexpected amalgamation of classy silver-leaf covered cabinet with remote-control TV is a real example of understated style that is easy to copy.**

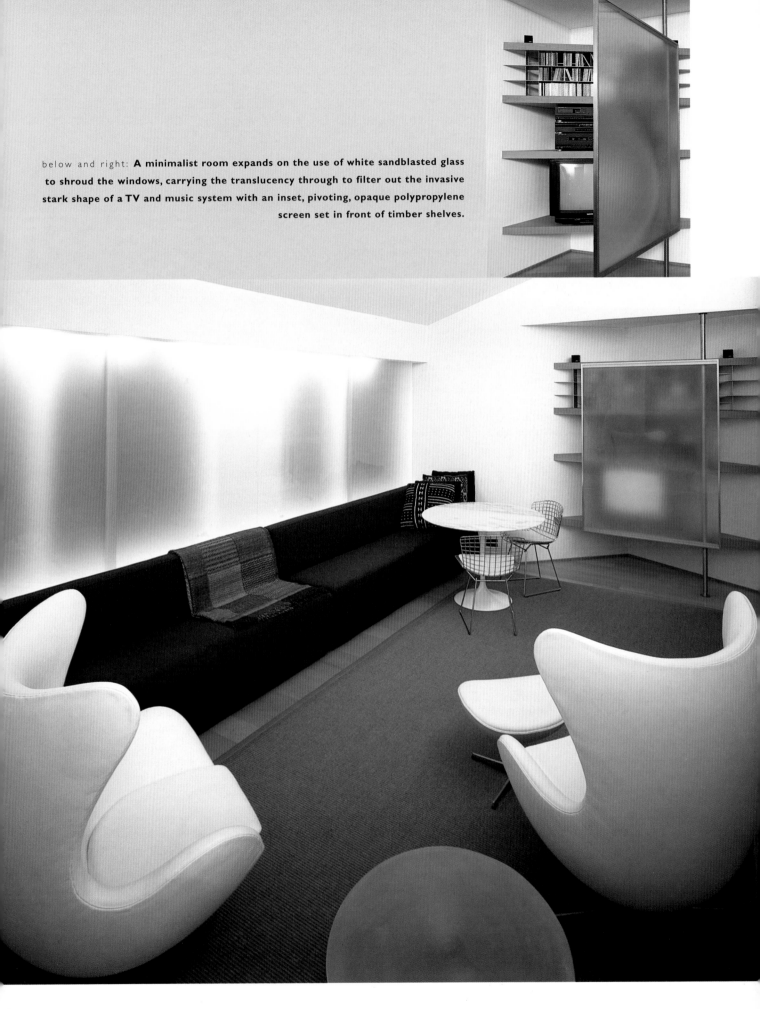

below and right: **A minimalist room expands on the use of white sandblasted glass to shroud the windows, carrying the translucency through to filter out the invasive stark shape of a TV and music system with an inset, pivoting, opaque polypropylene screen set in front of timber shelves.**

the world
in one room

Bland box-shaped rooms make most of us want to run a mile. But wait. Catch hold of your breath for a few minutes. A space like this is an opportunity for you to transform the room into something to fit your taste.

The owners of this living room were uncertain of how they wanted to modify the space, but they possessed one object that they loved: an Indian coffee table. From this one piece of furniture stemmed the idea of the world in one room. No longer would the room appear grey and cell-like. Instead, the owners would feel as if they had been on a trans-global trek without them ever having set foot on a plane. Clever shopping for some ethnic artefacts and the use of evocative colour schemes were all that was needed for the room to have universally appealing elegance.

right: **A screen doesn't have to look like a piece of Victoriana. The design of this eight-panelled screen is inspired by African tribal shields.** See page 183 for how to screen off a TV.

First, the elementary groundwork had to be completed. The uninspiring concrete floor needed a whole new look, which was achieved using battered old English oak floorboards from a salvage yard. Once they were laid, pampered and polished, we were well on the way to attaining the spirit of the room.

No room is complete without a fireplace – however hot the country. Disappointingly, when the existing aperture was exposed it was not central to the chimney breast, because the neighbour's flue ran on the right side. Obstacles like these should be looked at from a positive angle: an off-centre fireplace could look enchanting. An old Indonesian railway

right: **Using reclaimed floorboards is more environmentally friendly, and brings instant character to a featureless room.** See page 159 for how to lay reclaimed floorboards.

ethnic

above left: **Positioning lights
away from an original
electric point like this is a
great way of avoiding costly
re-channelling and is easy to
do** (see page 171).

above centre and right: **Cobbles placed
around the outside add an extra textural
quality to the glass bowl fire** (see page 180). **As
a finishing touch to the firescape, pebbles and
cacti were used to enhance the feeling of
desert winds in faraway places.**

sleeper with wonderful roughened edges (found on the same trip to the
salvage yard) formed a mantelpiece with characterful cracks and crevices
left exposed.

The chimney flue had been cemented internally and would have been
costly to open up, so a real fire was out of the question. A substitute
was called for. A glass bowl and electric light bulbs to give the sparkle
effect were an ingenious alternative.

If you don't want central lighting in a room but don't want the expense
of rewiring either, you could do what I did here and position three long,
tubular knitted lampshades towards the corner of the room, all powered
from the existing ceiling point. Silver chain hung from the same hooks as
the wire made a decorative feature of the looped wire. Hanging the lights
together not only looks tremendous but is also more cost-effective than
wiring up three separate lights. The oriental look of the knitted
shades was complemented by a tall, freestanding paper light, in the
opposite corner.

don't limit your horizons: think India, think Africa – think the world!

- Life shouldn't always be symmetrical: try an off-centre paint design.

- Don't dilute colour inspiration. Only cowards choose wishy-washy colours.

- If you can't have a real fire, then make your fireplace a decorative feature.

Now for the walls. Inspired by the colours and patterns of African tribal art, I created a contemporary western adaptation – using ready-mixed paint instead of natural dyes and pigments! The caramel-coloured walls were painted with blocks of cobalt blue and terracotta. Freehand squiggles in earth tones and finger-painted dots complete the look.

5 steps to a glorious global room

❶ **Look at books on international subjects for design inspiration.**

❷ **Check out junk shops and salvage yards for old ethnic items. New ones can be found in Chinese and Indian shops.**

❸ **Copy colour schemes from exotic travel postcards or from scraps of luscious fabrics from distant lands.**

❹ **Cross-cultural divides: mix Indian fabrics with Japanese paintings and African walls for a nomadic global style.**

❺ **Accessorize thoughtfully: select only the finest from each culture that you represent.**

far left: **Prickly cacti wrapped with Manila rope provide a textural contrast with natural linen cushions and a waffle throw.**

centre: **Colour blocking combined with freehand squiggles and finger paint forms a backdrop for a shelf unit** (see page 162 for how to paint an African design). **Together with the unusual light and chair, they make a contemporary still-life.**

left: **Venetian blinds provide a blank canvas for striking ginger lilies from the Caribbean and heliconias from Central Mexico.**

In keeping with the flavour of current internationalism, decorative objects were brought in from all four corners of the globe. Desert cacti, Peruvian pan pipes, flowers from Central America, English terracotta pots, oriental pictures and a French table resembling an African drum provided the perfect detailing.

A room without a focal point often feels rather sad, and a room without a fireplace can be sterile and uneasy. Somewhere deeply rooted in all of us is a primeval desire to huddle around flickering flames. And there is nothing quite like the warmth, comfort and satisfaction of a burning fire for giving a home its heart.

If a fireplace is open but redundant, be a little imaginative. This is the ideal space for creating striking displays, a mini-gallery. Don't just resort to a disgusting, tired old dried-flower arrangement. The mantelpiece, too, offers a wonderful exhibition opportunity that is under-utilized in most homes. Mantelpiece dressing almost always looks identical: a clock smack bang in the centre, with a pair of candlesticks on either side. So be brave and get rid of them, or, at the very least, place the candlesticks asymmetrically for a slightly quirkier look. Better still, find more interesting alternatives – ones which you can change regularly and seasonally – keeping not just the open fireplace alive, but the mantelpiece, too.

focal fireplaces

above: **A traditional fire surround gets a modern studded treatment to bring it up to date. Upholstery studs accentuate the architectural panels of the wooden surround. Treat the mantelpiece like a miniature landscape, with several favourite objects placed side by side. It's important though to get the scale of the objects right, or it will just look like a hotch-potch.**

right: **When is a log store not a log store? When it becomes a piece of art. This graphic, symmetrical fireplace layout looks spectacular and uses nothing more than an excess supply of logs which, when stacked to these limits, are sensational. The two elementary spotlights pick out the textural quality even when the fire is not alight.**

below and right: **Fire and ice – or at least a parody of it.** Here a simple fireplace is given the ultimate partner – glass. The glass mantelshelf (see page 180) with its undulating curves has been placed below the opening rather than above. Set alongside the contemporary chrome firebasket, the look is one of a seamless flow of grace, clarity and translucency. The glass hearth beneath reflects all the colours and shapes back up.

modern
country

Modernism
can be totally at home
with country life. An idyllic
rural hideaway isn't on the same
scale as an inner-city loft and does-
n't offer the same scope, but it can still
be decorated and furnished in a stylish,
glossy way. This living room situated deep
in the heart of the countryside amid rolling
green hills proves that country doesn't have
to mean quaint. Its owners yearned for the
peace and quiet of the countryside, but
wanted their home to accommodate their
taste for contemporary, urban
furniture. This room is as far
from typical chintz as I
could muster.

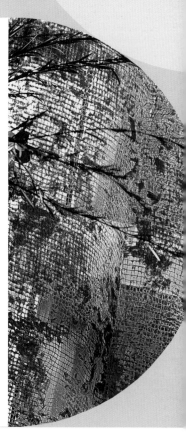

left: **The
cast-iron fire
surround was stripped
and polished to a glossy
lustre. Once its paint was
removed, it proved to be full of
intricate detail, providing a crisp
contrast with the sharp-edged
mustard yellow walls. It also makes
an unusual contrast to the room's
modern furniture. To its right,
chunky shelves** (see page 152) **hold
books, while a cupboard below
houses the music system.**

right: **Gauzy blue scrim at the
windows is an unexpected
touch which brings a soft,
luminous glow into
the room.**

below and inset: **The chimney breast is treated asymmetrically, with a cardboard-tube storage system on one side and shelves on the other. A freestanding bendy wooden screen loosens up the spirit of an otherwise boxy room.** See page 152 for how to make cardboard tube storage.

space light colour texture detail

Imagine decorating your living room with radiance, glow and shine, or giving it contrast, sparkle and luminescence. What kind of mystical paint would you use? Well, none. All of these qualities and many more come from one medium: light. Intangible though it is, light is one of the most powerful decorating tools ever.

Living room light must be all things to all householders. Most living rooms need a variable pattern of lighting, which adapts to your requirements at specific times of the day or for different pursuits. Natural light in a living room should be energizing without the sun baking you alive. If direct sunlight is too strong, then diffuse it through fine fabric drapes or venetian blinds to tone down its intensity to a more manageable glow. Used well, electric light can be a formidable aid to room decoration. The way to illuminate your space succesfully is to voyage around the room, thinking which details – a picture or favourite object – to pick out. Then decide whether to light them from above with a spotlight, midway with a table lamp or up from the floor. Light need not come just from overhead.

living room light

left: **Light fantastic. Exquisite lighting forms the central part of this living room. Two overhead spotlights illuminate alcoves on either side of the chimney breast, where ornate laurel wreath wall lights give decorative symmetry. The glass fascia of the chimney breast glows with a series of four downlighters placed behind the glass.**

right: **A warehouse living space is flooded with unbounded sunlight, left to flow through large, undressed windows. Overhead, halogen lights are fitted to a suspended track system which snakes across the room, providing more directional light when needed.**

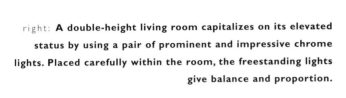
right: **A double-height living room capitalizes on its elevated status by using a pair of prominent and impressive chrome lights. Placed carefully within the room, the freestanding lights give balance and proportion.**

eating

Think about **where and how you**

eat. The days of a room just for dining are

long gone. Today's **eating zones can**

offer visual enticements as

well as gastronomic ones — whether it's a

lively kitchen or the TV.

slim
and stylish

Kitchens frequently have a sober demeanour. They may contain all the vital working elements, but often look more dreary than you could imagine. What you want is a kitchen design that sizzles. A room with superstar status. My own kitchen has the added problem of being long and narrow, so I introduced some lean lines and natural organic shapes to break up the tunnel effect.

The cost of real limestone on the floor was prohibitive, but colourwashed MDF cut into irregular contours was an inventive alternative.

Simple Shaker-style birch units were personalized by fitting perforated aluminium panels into the door frames and by attaching more contemporary handles.

Finally, to emphasize the ceiling and the airiness of the room, walls and ceiling were divided into blocks of colour. The result is a kitchen that combines the natural with the industrial, hard lines with soft curves, and rich, dark colours with brightness and light.

below left: **The curvy worktop** (see page 166) **and splashback are both made from laminate bonded to birch ply. The fake limestone floor** (see page 161) **is a lot less expensive.**

below centre: **Perforated aluminium sheets give ordinary units a cool, semi-industrial feel** (see page 167).

below right: **Smooth and streamlined, this suspended table** (see page 177) **makes an ideal spot for breakfast.**

below: **Windows play a leading role in creating this bright airy space. The bold paint design draws attention to the sloping ceiling, and not even the French doors get in its way!**

See page 164 for how to paint up and over colour.

space light colour texture detail

Wouldn't it be great if every kitchen was the perfect shape and the size of your local town hall, with an army of restaurant staff churning out meals at your every whim? Reality — for most of us, anyway — is a kitchen that is barely bigger than an understairs cupboard. If your kitchen is also an awkward shape, it can make even the best of us tear our hair out. But I'm a great believer in always searching for the positive side of a tricky situation. Good planning is the key to a successful kitchen no matter how troublesome the room shape.

odd-shaped kitchens

Irksome kitchens aren't just the small ones, either. In a large room, it can be difficult to know where to start when creating a workable layout. A perfect plan is not, in itself, a recipe for success. You are better placed than anyone else to know your kitchen requirements. Decide where to site a cooking area, washing facilities and where's best for the fridge. Once you've determined these, the other components should fall into place. If the room is shaped oddly, think more laterally but keep the ergonomics working. Leave space to move around so that you don't cramp your style.

above: **A tiny annexe at the rear of a house has had the barrier walls torn down, opening the kitchen, rather than tucking it away. The cooker is set at a slight angle, defining the entry to the kitchen, while the units, walls and ceiling are painted a soothing cream colour to help them recede. Ceiling panels following the length of the room also help to create a sense of depth.**

right: **Some imagination is called for when a kitchen also has to act as a busy thoroughfare. This swanky galley kitchen skilfully allows access on the right-hand side to the adjoining living zones. The island's central units are fitted with stunning fluidly shaped glass worktops and splashback, which give the feeling that that one can walk unencumbered from kitchen area to living zone.**

above and left: **A staircase coming up into the centre of the kitchen is an unusual challenge, but is a chance to create something truly special. Here, the stairwell is hidden, but its surrounding curved wall of galvanized metal fitted with a series of display shelves is the room's focal point. The dining table on wheels doubles up as a good-sized working desk, made to fit into the curved wall when it is not being used.**

survival of the unfitted

The unfitted kitchen is not a new concept, more a revisiting of an old idea. Before the 1950s, all kitchens were kitted out with freestanding tables, cookers and larders. Then along came a new concept – the fitted kitchen – which changed kitchens for ever (or so we thought). Now, 50 years later, things have come full circle and unfitted is back in vogue.

below left and right:
Scaffolding around the sink (see page 156) makes the washing-up zone look as if it could be moved to another part of the room, but it's just an illusion.

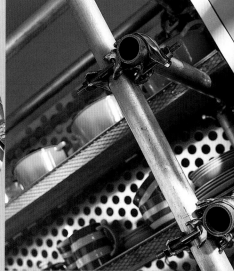

centre: Flatpack shelving like this offers more food storage space than standard kitchen units. The shapes of kitchen objects were cut out of MDF to make a delicious alternative to standard doors. You could adapt the idea for other rooms if you wanted – for instance, using cut-outs of bath paraphernalia for bathroom cupboards, or office bits and bobs for a home study storage area.

Here to stay and all set to make a big impact in the twenty-first century, unfitted means freedom and flexibility in kitchen design. No longer fixed to one spot, many functional elements are suddenly movable. Now you can have kitchen units that, with a great leap of the imagination, can practically jog around the room.

At the couture end of the market, unfitted kitchens come with pretty hefty price tags, but this clever adaptation shows that an affordable version isn't just on the horizon - it's a reality.

space light colour texture detail

above: **Thanks to the two movable food preparation trolleys
either side, the cooker and its space-age extractor hood look
as if they're movable too. You almost expect them to take off!**

steps to a fab unfitted kitchen

5

❶ Be ruthless and cut down to the bare essentials. The unfitted kitchen will offer marginally less storage space, but that should be outweighed by its attractiveness and flexibility.

❷ The watch-word is mobility: units with castors and worktops that can be raised or lowered. Make sinks and cookers freestanding and they'll blend quite happily with the unfitted look.

❸ Designate different work zones for washing-up, cooking, eating and storage for ease of operation.

❹ Industrial materials and open shelves add to the 'I'm only stopping for a moment' effect.

❺ Don't ignore walls, floors and windows: they will be much more exposed in an unfitted kitchen and will need to make an impact.

below left: **Everything in the kitchen adds to the sense of fluidity and mobility. Even the walls behind the cooker are undulating, made from bendy plywood fitted onto a framework** (see page 165).

The first step - as always - is to divide the kitchen into activity zones. Because of the plumbing, the washing-up zone has to be permanently fixed, but the scaffolding structure around it makes it look almost movable. To add to the effect, the area underneath the sink is left open, so the drainage pipe, waste bin and freestanding drawer unit are visible. The cooking theatre is so dramatic, it really lives up to its hoi polloi name. It's made from four key elements: a freestanding stainless-steel cooker, an over-head extractor unit, and two modular food preparation trolleys.

kitchens a go-go

centre and left: **The cutting edge of kitchen design. The beautiful organic textures of cool concrete and wood make these work surfaces very special.**

right: An unfitted kitchen has the bonus that most of what is in it can be taken with you if you move. Here only the sink and cooker are fixed. The rest can lead a nomadic lifestyle if you do.

right: **The glass of the windows was replaced with sandblasted glass in modernist circle shapes. Sandblasting or acid-etching a design onto an otherwise ordinary window adds interior-design appeal as well as privacy.** See page 169 for how to etch on glass.

move it

Like the sink, the cooker can't be movable, but the trolleys either side are, so the effect is almost the same. With trolleys like these, you can chop in one part of the kitchen, then whisk the trolleys over to the washing-up zone.

The table under the window is supremely versatile. It can be used as a worktop or breakfast bar or, when lowered and moved out on its castors, it becomes the dining table for six that the owners wanted. Its top is covered with a mosaic, adding yet another layer of texture to the room.

All in all, a state-of-the-art kitchen with attitude. And the best part is that it can be taken with you if you move!

nuggets + no-nos

● Define the floor space with rubber or lino flooring in contrasting colours.

● You won't find this look at a kitchen showroom. Instead head for a good builder's merchants to get all the different components.

above: **Now you see it, now you don't. The dining table, with its beautiful mosaic tiles in electric blues, takes centre stage when it's pulled out from beneath the window.**

left: **The washing machine and fridge-freezer are housed in a metropolitan-style unit with a pitched roof. Perforated aluminium sheeting fixed to the wall alongside holds extra cookery paraphernalia.**

below: **Go catering style and display your kitchenware with pride rather than hide it away from prying eyes. The 'at a glance' crockery is effortlessly accessed from easy-glide mesh drawers fitted to these restaurant-inspired stainless-steel trolleys.**

These days most of us shop weekly or fortnightly, while other enviably organized mortals may put themselves through trolley traumas only once a month. This kind of forward planning is admirable but requires an abundance of storage space in the kitchen, for both fresh and non-perishable foods. You may have to consider putting an additional bank of cupboards in another room or hallway. But even if you have a huge utility annexe, you'll still need to allocate space efficiently for crockery, cutlery, glasses, and pots and pans.

kitchen storage

below: **One entire wall of this tranquil-looking kitchen conceals the reality of cooking hustle and bustle. A series of Japanese-style sliding screen doors hides vast amounts of storage for food and equipment. The design of the doors is echoed in the white laminate and blonde wood drawers below the work surfaces.**

Display versus hideaway is a common predicament of kitchen storage. A combination of the two makes a more attractive kitchenscape, but bear in mind that what's on display should be aesthetically pleasing. However, with the fabulous decorative labelling of today's foodstuffs, it doesn't have to be your best china. Efficient use of space is the key to successful kitchen storage. So if your fridge sneaks open of its own accord, take it as a sign that you need a bigger one – or stop buying so many ready-made meals!

below: **An air of quiet simplicity pervades in this large kitchen. The most frequently used condiments are placed on open beech shelves for quick decision-making – a halogen spotlight is angled overhead for clear viewing, night or day. The extra long birch- and marble-topped island unit has two elongated sliding doors, painted bubble-gum pink, concealing all manner of other kitchen equipment.**

kitsch
kitchen

Once upon a time, kitchens came in white, beige, or beige-coloured wood. Now the time has come to have a sense of humour, don your sunglasses and muster your courage. We present the Kitsch Kitchen in full Technicolor, as they say in the movies! With a few clever ideas and buckets of bravado, you can turn a perfectly serviceable but bland kitchen into a sparkly million-dollar looker that certainly stands out from the crowd – and doesn't take a trip to the bank manager to put into action.

below left: **This very ordinary basic kitchen cried out for a change. Not any old change, but one that bears no resemblance to a serious cook's kitchen. That's not to say that its amusing design doesn't turn out some serious recipes!**

below right: **Having a 'Wizard of Oz' approach doesn't mean you can't have a working kitchen. An abundance of crockery storage and acres of worktop space are incorporated in the wacky design.** See page 166 for how to make a curvy worktop.

If you want to transform your kitchen, you don't always need to get involved in the trauma of major structural changes. Why not make the best of what you've got? Think imaginatively and laterally. A few bright paint colours and some fun fixtures and fittings can do wonders for dull decor.

What makes this kitchen eye-popping is not its layout but the colour scheme. It might make sober citizens shudder with fear, but you can easily repaint any catastrophic clashes.

below centre: **Eating will certainly never be boring again at this sign-of-the-times eating pod** (see page 176).

space light colour texture detail

You don't have to be mad to like the floor, but it certainly helps! Circles of various sizes and colours created a fabulous soap-suddy design, turning an otherwise dull cork floor into a show-stopping focal point. Buy a selection of sample paint pots to help you choose colours before going with the real thing.

With so many lively colours in the room, it's important to have stabilizing black and white some-where in the scheme. So the old school chairs were turned into zebras with pink legs! The windows were left undressed – there's plenty to distract the eye – but they were framed with decorative fretwork painted shocking pink for some zest.

below: **The original panelled kitchen unit doors were retained but modernized with laminated sheets** (see page 167). **New wavy door handles were attached to groove up the look.**

right: **Precut wooden fretwork trim can be bought at most DIY stores. A perfect finishing touch for windows, it can also be used to give a decorative edge to splashback tiles.**

left: **Nothing escaped becoming a talking point – not even the dishwasher and washing machine. They were rescued from normality by a wacky hand-painted bubble design.** See page 166 for how to paint a household appliance.

right: **Why have an ordinary cork-tiled floor when you can have this zany one?** See page 160 for how to lay cork tiles; and page 158 for how to paint a kitsch kitchen floor.

above left: **The shelves above the worktop were cut to a wavy design similar to that of the work surfaces. Chrome poles were used for extra support for heavy weights.**

Wavy worktops and shelves demonstrate that, like people, not everything in life is straight. Why, oh why are we always so regimented in our homes? A kitchen worktop that literally flows around you is such a pleasure to work at, especially if, like me, you need lots of encouragement to venture into the kitchen in the first place!

The Kitsch Kitchen is guaranteed to appeal to young children – who knows, they might love being in it so much that they'll learn to do the washing up!

nuggets + no-nos

● **If you have young children, attempt this room only if you're happy to have all their friends around to play in it.**

● **A kitchen isn't all about food. Don't forget space for watching TV, paying the bills – and playing, of course!**

centre and above right: **The laminated leopard-print surface for the curvy worktops continued the animal theme.**

if you want to
be **taken seriously**
in the neighbourhood,
don't attempt this
kitchen!

Startling contemporary kitchen design, creating bold, exciting spaces and textures, is re-defining our notion of kitchen surfaces. Gutsy and sculptural, freely mixing the industrial with the domestic, today's look is nothing short of awe-inspiring. In a kitchen, texture goes beyond being a feast for your eyes. When preparing food, there is a wonderful physical interaction between produce and products. And by juxtaposing surfaces with unexpected and unrelated materials – rough concrete and smooth glass, shiny steel with grainy wood – you can create a series of textural transitions even in the tiniest of spaces.

But texture goes beyond the realms of granite worktops and a wooden chopping board. Much of the visual strength of a kitchen comes when you have clearly defined zones for cooking, eating and so on. Over-co-ordinated doors, worktops and paintwork can frequently look yawningly boring. So think vertically as well as horizontally. Walls, floors, divisions, windows and ceilings all play a large part in the creation of spectacular textural effects.

kitchen texture

above: **This kitchen landscape has been created with clean lines set at opposing orientations. Viewed from across the kitchen table, the louvred windows and beamed ceiling form a network of horizontal and vertical planes in contrasting paint, wood and glass finishes. The wall-mounted cooking and washing-up zone stands out with its facing of jumbled broken black and white tiles.**

right: **A kitchen decorated with conservative caution uses the varying heights and textures of worktops and ledges to create visual interest. Matt grey laminate, rich, cherry-coloured varnished wood, flat white walls and wine-coloured glossy ceramic tiles form an understated textural design.**

right: **Old meets new. An old -style cooking range sits at close quarters with a polished chrome sink bowl, itself set into a glamorous glass worktop. Overhead, a metallic wire rack suspended from the ceiling offers oodles of space to store an array of glossy kitchen pots and pans.**

below: **The effect of the large curved wall of slate tiles, a material normally used outside, is lavish and tactile. The grey slate is off-set by blonde wood, orange walls, brushed chrome appliances, shiny red vinyl chairs and an opaque glass table. A hotbed of kitchen textural innovation.**

integr

Capsule living – one room, one

function – has **no place** in the home of

the future. Changing lifestyles demand

radical alterations. Create

combination spaces that **allow a**

room to evolve, adapting to

the various activities that occur within a day.

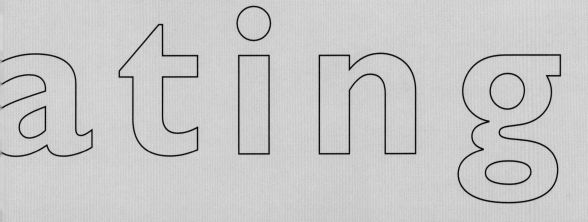

jack-in-the-box

Living in a house the size of a shoebox would test
most of us to the limit. But try fitting all facets of
daily life into just one room. Then, to make you
swallow even harder, consider how exposed and audible
all aspects of your life would be. A tiny wee space
needn't be a Lilliputian nightmare, however. It can be
a little gem, offering more intimacy and sense of
refuge than an airport-sized flat ever could.

   The classic mistake with one-room living is to
believe that it will do for now. If you go down this
road, it won't feel like home and you'll be suicidal
within days. Instead, treat your petite pad as a
palace. Use the best your money can buy. Go for
glamour and chic, with the most comfortable bed and
the loudest alarm clock you can find, and the best
chef or, failing that, the best microwave you can
afford. Multi-functional and portable furniture is the
key, but only buy a sofabed if it's for guests - for
regular use it has absolutely no sex appeal!

below: **With a plain cream
colour base you can add
lively pictures or large-scale
abstract art painted directly
onto the walls or cupboards.**

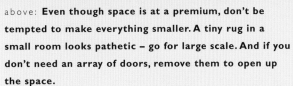

above: **Even though space is at a premium, don't be tempted to make everything smaller. A tiny rug in a small room looks pathetic – go for large scale. And if you don't need an array of doors, remove them to open up the space.**

left: **In studio living, every square inch of space has to be utilized, and furniture has to have dual function wherever possible. Here, a dining room chair is put to good use in the office area.**

space light colour texture detail

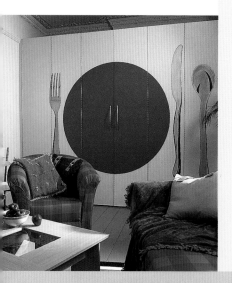

This chameleon studio had to metamorphose into its different guises as the day progressed: an office by day, a living/dining area in the evening and a bedroom at night. Oh, and a cooking area at any time! The first step was to compartmentalize, organize and store in containers hidden from view anything not being used. Cluttered mini-rooms, where all the activities take place together, just don't work. All this might mean that, unless you are a minimalist by nature, you have to pare down your belongings.

above: **Hinged screening panels hide the kitchen from sight when not being used. Just in case the owner forgets where his kitchen is after a late night out, there's a giant place setting to remind him!**

right: **The budget jade-coloured unit doors were spruced up by painting in a central panel of peppermint, the shade also used to paint the fridge and washing machine for a unified look.**

The kitchen was relocated in a narrow recess along an entire wall. With kitchen appliances and unsightly debris, it was the one area that, left unscreened, would look most out of place. The problem was solved by installing huge floor-to-ceiling concertina doors, which simply pull back to reveal a fully working kitchen. And one quick tug back again renders that dreaded pile of washing-up out of sight, out of mind. The layout of the kitchen was kept simple and linear, with few appliances on show.

left: **Safety glass, a builders' basic, was used as a splashback. It allowed the colour of the wall to show through, while still protecting it. Glass is also very hygienic as it's so easy to wipe clean.**

below: **Stainless-steel laminate worktops and colours reminiscent of a 1950s American diner give this tiny studio kitchen an extra special feel.**

pop up

A toning 1950s colour scheme helped maintain the kitchen's streamlined look. The ceilings, walls and woodwork were painted in one shade of cream, a warmer colour than white, which can look grey and dingy in low light. And, to carry on the sense of unity, the floorboards of the entire room were painted a single bright blue. One large rug added a touch of comfort.

Corners can easily become dead areas. Not so in this studio, where every inch of space had to have a function. Here, the corner was fitted with a cupboard with an integral fake fireplace to give the living area a strong focal point. Originally a music system and TV were seated on a low table, spilling their cables, discs and tapes into the room. Now the corner cupboard houses this electronic bedlam. Each door panel in the cupboard is simply pushed to gain access to the piece of gadgetry behind. Open all the panels and you've got the complete entertainment system. Close them for the more laid-back fireplace.

below left: **The coffee table looks simple enough, but with an extra large tabletop and a few cushions from the sofa, it can seat six for elegant Japanese-style dining. When not in use, the top can easily be stashed away in a cupboard.**

below right: **The doors of the corner cupboard are all different sizes, fitting together neatly like the pieces of a jigsaw puzzle.** See page 151 for how to make a clever corner unit.

inset: **Lots of decorative lights in a small room can clutter up the space. Run-of-the-mill light shades – with a little carpentry help – now look striking, while spreading light more evenly around the room.** See page 171 for how to make an arc light.

5 steps to fab one room living

❶ See double. Give everything in the room two purposes wherever possible.

❷ Keep things undercover or behind closed doors. A wall bed is a must and use doors or screens to mask off the kitchen area.

❸ Streamline your possessions and get rid of any objects you don't truly love. You need only five key pieces of furniture in the living area: a small round table (which will seat people more than a square one), two dining chairs, a sofa, an armchair, and a coffee table.

❹ Be creative to utilize every available space. Things will need to be stored unobtrusively in every nook and cranny. And be tidy – clear away any evidence of one activity before moving on to another.

❺ Simpify the decor. One floor finish throughout makes the area seem larger. And don't go for a multitude of patterns on rugs, sofas and curtains or you'll soon want to throw them out of the nearest window.

plan it well or life will be hell

right: **This super-slim workzone contains everything that the net surfer needs. Instead of drawers, brightly coloured shoeboxes under the desk give ample storage for computer disks and complete the snazzy look.** See page 179 for how to build a desk in a tight spot.

A narrow area by the entrance door became the workzone. A slide-out shelf for the computer keyboard could be pushed back again when not in use. The monitor was mounted on a bracket, which freed up the desk area for paperwork. A memoboard painted directly onto the wall with blackboard paint was more fun than an unsightly office-type noticeboard. Building the slender shelving unit for stationery and books right into the corner made it much less conspicuous, as it would be seen only side on from almost every angle in the room.

Behind the colourful graphics of the central doors lay the bedroom solution. Open the doors and, hey presto! Down comes one full-size double bed in all its glory. The bed was wall- and floor-mounted and sprung so that it would be as easy to get up as it is to get down. And the bedding could be held in place with two straps, so there was no need to have it stored anywhere else.

nuggets + no-nos

It sounds obvious, but before you buy any furniture, measure it to see if it will fit when you get it home.

A good extractor fan for your kitchen area is a necessity, so that you don't end up breathing in the stale aromas of your cooking while lying in bed.

above: **One...two...three! The cosy bedroom cubby hole comes with all the necessary fittings, including an integral light fitting. There are wardrobes on either side of the bed, and the higher ones contain pull-down jacket rails for easy access.**

Divide and conquer or go free flow. The conventional home is no longer wholly suited to many

of the demands of today's living. Overlapping functions are what we want – workspaces

merging with living spaces, living rooms alongside dining rooms, dining rooms next to cooking

zones. To achieve this, the most sensible and desirable option is transformable space. It's time

to tear the walls down and install things that think they're walls but are in fact movable

panels. Try walls that glide out on rolling castors or hinged panels that fold out origami-style.

Room dividing is the New-Age option.

Movable partitions enable the opening up of

grandiose expanses full of spatial fluidity, while still

allowing the creation of smaller intimate spaces

within. The result will be simple yet complex, with

continually changing perspectives.

dividing spaces

left: **A large swivelling sheet-metal partition
negates the need for a conventional hallway in this
contemporary apartment. Fitted with a single
industrial castor at one end and a pole fixed to the
ceiling at the other, the partition pivots a full
180 degrees, allowing the front door annexe to be
closed off completely while simultaneously giving
the adjoining room a radically new character.**

above: **With a graphic abstract slash through its centre, a movable arc-shaped burr-wood room divider gives a cheeky hint of what's beyond. Attached to the wall by means of three hinges, a single castor fixed to the bottom is positioned so the divider remains well balanced when it is moved.**

left: **A loft-style apartment is divided by a screen that is part-solid, part-transparent. It consists of a framework of fixed birch plywood sheets, held in place on the floor with metal strips and yacht rigging for extra support. This incorporates a central grid structure of glass and metal which glides open to create an uninterrupted space.**

all mapped
out

This dining room is a room for all reasons. A consortium of eating space, travel agent's and office in a house owned by a couple whose work constantly takes them abroad. The room also had to be designed with access to the staircase in mind.

The budget for doing up the room was minuscule, so some cost-cutting ideas were needed for providing the necessities. That doesn't stop you from making them that bit special, though. If you are planning a multi-purpose room like this one, spend some time weighing up what its principle uses are to be, and where you have no choice but to splash out. Here, the only items that cost much were the dining chairs.

Paint is always an inexpensive way of adding character. Here black and white squares were painted at intervals around the room over acidic lime-green and bold turquoise. The mood continues with broken black and white tiles revamping the fireplace.

right: **A fireplace often needs nothing more than a new insert to bring it to life. Broken black and white tiles are a very inexpensive way of achieving this** (see page 181).

space light colour texture detail

above: **A set of shelves doubles up as a work area. These chunky shelves are not difficult to make** (see page 152) **and look especially good because no fixtures are visible.**

above: **Get intimately acquainted with the world over dinner. This table was made from a door with legs attached. A world map was glued on top – you could use a poster or a painting – and a sheet of glass placed over it for protection.**

left: **Another space-saving idea: when wall space is at a premium, don't overlook the window area. This acrylic message board** (see page 175) **is hung over the window but still lets the light in.**

The small home office area snugly fitting between the window and the fireplace is nothing more than a few chunky shelves with one deeper shelf acting as the desk, but it serves its purpose for dealing with travel arrangements and paying household bills. Framed clear acrylic suspended in front of the venetian blinds becomes an at-a-glance, daily message board. A small galvanized metal drawer cabinet sits under the window to provide extra office storage. It's fitted with castors for instant mobility.

When more elbow room is required for making travel plans, the six-seater dining table – made from a door! – doubles up as a project desk and huge world route planner map. The table is set at an angle in the room rather than straight and square, to make sure there is comfortable access to all areas of the room, and especially to the staircase.

A revolution is taking place: the office has come home to roost so now working from home is the way to do business. It's time to turn that weary spare room or understairs nook into an inspiring workspace, where a crust can be earned and the bills paid. But don't work in a spot where, with one swivel of your chair, you're confronted by a monumental heap of washing-up or ironing. Choose a location where you can concentrate and that has generous daylight and the possibility of plenty of storage space, then differentiate between office and domestic drudgery with screens or doors. And don't try to recreate a bland city office within your home. This is your chance to reflect your personality, to add colour, and to soften the blow of work by surrounding yourself with comfort.

working spaces

right: **Nowadays the traditional frontiers between where we work and where we live are becoming very fuzzy. In a room that has to serve as both office and sleeping area, the buzzword is containment. Here a simple worktop desk runs along one wall from door to window while opposite, the bed is raised, leaving space for storage of files below.**

above: **A chic guest room doubles up as a stylish home office.
To stay one step ahead of the paper trail and bring a sense of
order, the room boasts a fully fitted storage unit with integral
lighting illuminating the desk area. A plush dual-purpose sofa
turns into a single bed for guest use.**

right: **If virginal minimalism requires too much iron will, then
simple understated lines and shapes can give the same air of
polished efficiency. In this contemporary home a gently curved
desk has been imaginatively positioned around a feature
wall. For simplicity's sake, the desk is fixed directly to the wall
and stands on a single chrome leg.**

one-room living

This ingenious studio flat is a microcosm of any normal home fitted into a space barely large enough to turn around in. Despite its mere 17 square metres (180 sq ft), it has a startling number of living pockets cleverly carved out of it, making it feel almost like a ship's cabin. The studio works so well thanks to the use of different horizontal levels maximizing the space and to the sense of unity in the decoration. Furniture has been kept to a minimum everywhere, with unexpected hiding places provided for the usual household clutter.

The purpose-built units have enabled the corner-nook kitchen to be fully equipped with a fridge, microwave, conventional hob, waste disposal and food storage area – a remarkable accomplishment in such a minute space. Sitting alongside the compact kitchen is the living section, kitted out with display shelving, cupboards and a small bench sofa. The seat pad can be removed to reveal even more storage space. At one end of the room a full-length mirror cannily enlarges the whole space.

The mezzanine floor fearlessly cuts right across the flat's main window, allowing the light entering here to be shared between the upper and lower levels. A steep wooden staircase cleverly concealing extra storage space has been chosen rather than a ladder to lead up to the bedroom.

below: **The solid structure of the staircase is all part of the space-saving plan. Behind its electric-blue door a whole new world is revealed – a large cubby-hole for crockery.**

above: **The living quarters contain no excess furniture. Everything has to be stowed away and ship-shape.**

left: **Despite its size, this kitchen nevertheless manages to look stylish while containing all a cook needs to rustle up some gourmet food.**

space light colour texture detail

above: **At the end of the bedroom, an orange cupboard looks so simple you'd think it was a wall, but just one swish of a sliding door reveals a broad but shallow wardrobe large enough to take plenty of clothing.**

The galleried bedroom contains a further succession of essentials and daily comforts - bed, sofa and storage space. There's even room for a desk area on the platform overlooking the entrance hall. The mattress and the red sofa both sit directly above the ceiling below, while the greater headroom offered by the walkway was achieved by lowering the ceiling above the dining area. All in all, a miniature miracle.

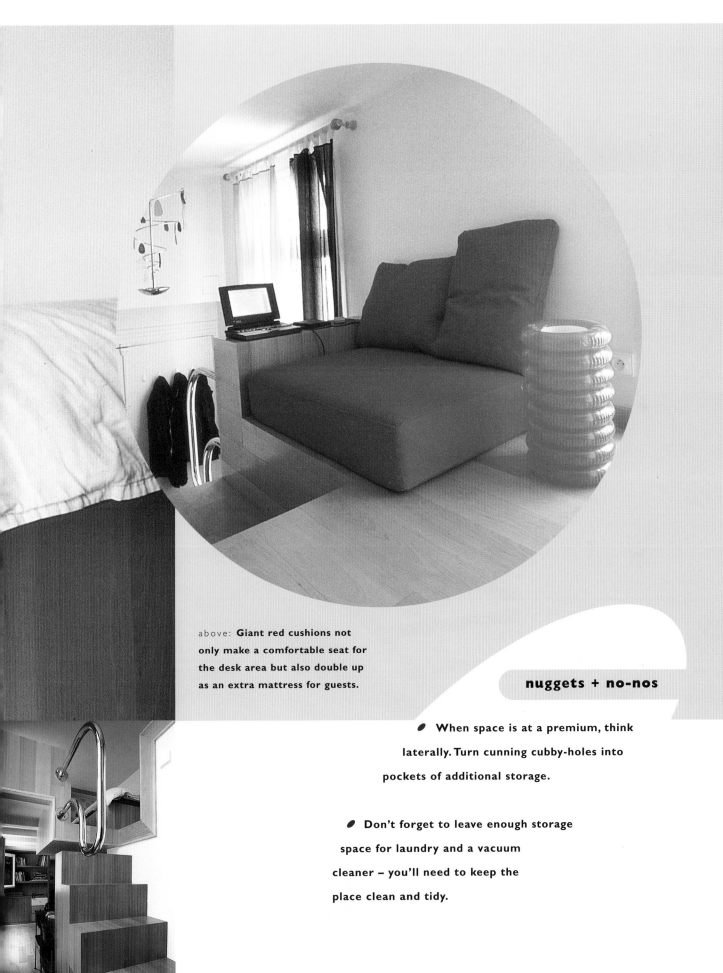

above: **Giant red cushions not
only make a comfortable seat for
the desk area but also double up
as an extra mattress for guests.**

nuggets + no-nos

When space is at a premium, think
laterally. Turn cunning cubby-holes into
pockets of additional storage.

Don't forget to leave enough storage
space for laundry and a vacuum
cleaner – you'll need to keep the
place clean and tidy.

Adding a second level is like creating an extra room. It can practically double the floorspace – invaluable in tiny areas that make you yearn for extra elbow room. But an astute second level is equally suited to grandiose, lofty expanses which hanker after a little more definition. In a large area, the new level can play host to one or more bedrooms, a study zone or even a bathroom. Not only is it worthwhile from the aesthetic point of view to put yourself through

raised
areas

the nightmare of building a second level, but the added value it will bring to your home should compensate for any initial misgivings.

In small rooms use the layering method to produce different zones within the same room. The most common way of achieving this is by building a sleeping platform so the bed is above eye level, out of sight and out of mind. The area below can then be freed up for use for storage, as a work station or for bathing.

above: **A small studio multiplies its floor space with the skilful use of levels. A platform bedroom sits directly above the kitchen and the staircase has also been put to good use. With every step there is a storage cupboard or drawer.**

right: **Country living without a hint of saccharine. A confidently erected timber platform makes an architectural statement in a large open space. The grand-scale heavy-duty legs with steel brackets and wooden framework have been left bare so you can look in awe at the magnificent construction.**

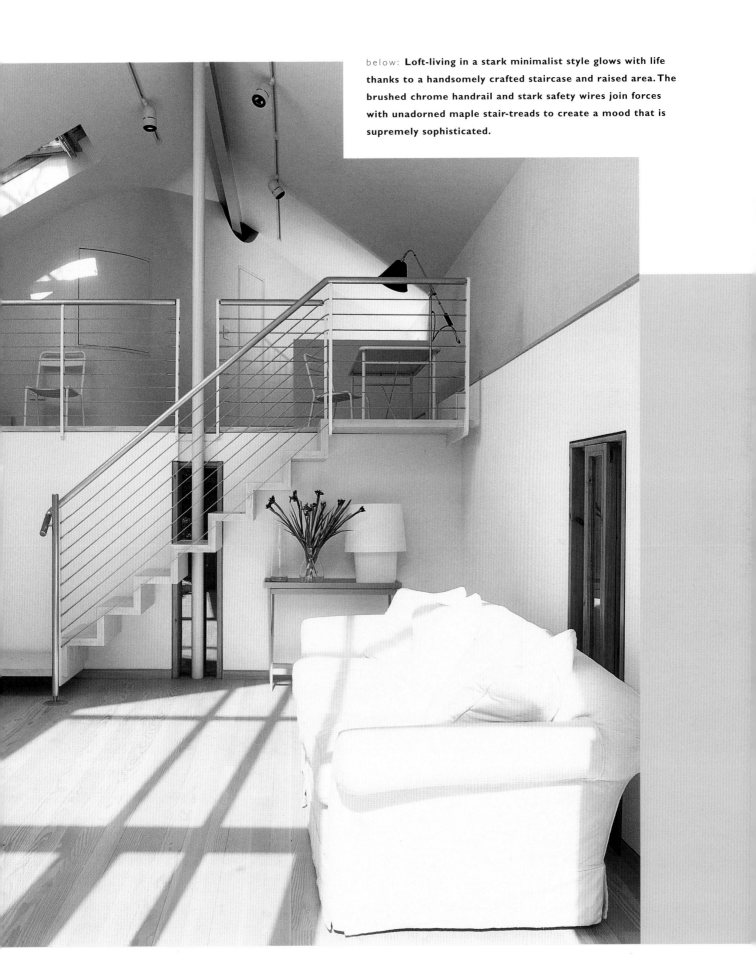

below: **Loft-living in a stark minimalist style glows with life thanks to a handsomely crafted staircase and raised area. The brushed chrome handrail and stark safety wires join forces with unadorned maple stair-treads to create a mood that is supremely sophisticated.**

bathin

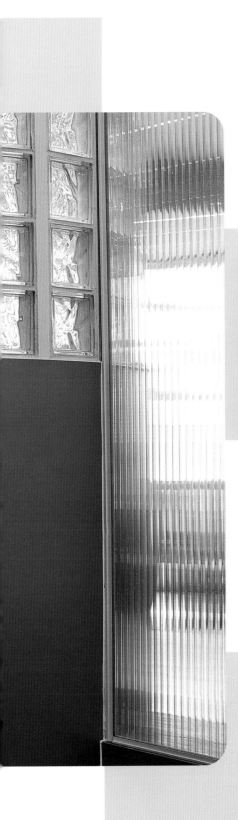

Your bathroom will most probably be the

smallest room in the home, but it can also be

the most **self-indulgent.** Turn it into

a comfort zone where **warmth, style**

and luxury prevail. A shower

needn't be a dribble from a clogged-up

shower-head — it can become a **total**

wet experience.

small but
perfectly formed

above: **An arrangement of one large and five small oval-shaped mirrors ensures that no part of your body escapes reflection!**

Small bathrooms often suffer from the visible calamity of content over style. Once you have jigged in the basic necessities, there is hardly any space (or energy!) left for artistic expression. My bathroom is tiny but I refused to get steamed up. I decided to make a splash in an understated way, putting all my efforts into creating a room of soothing natural tones and irresistible tactile appeal. I've tried all the latest products for walls, floors and surfaces, but sometimes, the inexpensive basics are best, especially if your bank account says so.

The bath, toilet and washbasin were repositioned to make better use of the small space. One treat was a new wall-hung washbasin, inspired by an ammonite. Wall-hung fixtures trick the brain into thinking a room is bigger than it actually is.

right: **A splendid chrome monobloc tap with a blue perspex top sets off this basin wonderfully. The blue colour is picked out again in the toilet seat and towels.**

opposite: **Shutters with ovals cut out of larger ovals create an unusual design.** See page 168 for how to make fretwork shutters.

inset: **You can customize a standard light pull using stones from the beach. Simply thread the string of the light pull through the natural holes in the stones, and tie a knot at one end to secure them.**

space light colour texture detail

touch it

The walls were screened with simple vertical wooden battens fixed in a strict pattern to create wonderful pockets of light and shade. Instead of the usual single mirror, oval-shaped mirrors were placed randomly above the washbasin. This oval shape was carried through to the bespoke shutters.

above: **The bath was revitalized with sleek new chrome fittings and a lovely cobbled surround.**

right: **Laying vinyl tiles is a cheap way of transforming the floor and is easy to do** (see page 160).

right: **The glass door of the bathroom cabinet was given an acid-etched look with the aid of a spray can** (see page 169).

below: **Screen your walls with simple battens for a more textural look** (see page 162).

A large glass-fronted living room cupboard made an overly generous bathroom cabinet, but it was customized by decorating the glass door to give an acid-etch effect.

A tiny floor space should still make a big impact. Laminated vinyl flooring with a photographically transferred pattern of stone and cobbles makes a bold splash and brings the whole bathroom to a cohesive textural conclusion.

nuggets + no-nos

● If you can't afford to decorate, just change details such as towels, vases, pots, pictures, taps and window dressing.

● Another way to give your bathroom a facelift while keeping costs down is to hang on to your sanitary ware, but reposition it.

below: **A completely mirrored wall doubles the sense of space and is the key to this bathroom. White mosaic tiles glide across the floor, up the side of the bath and onto the walls. A rudimentary sheet of glass makes a shower screen, while a stainless-steel countertop slung from the bath edge to the opposite wall supports a matching surface-mounted washbasin.**

One miraculous transparent substance with a multitude of uses dominates bathrooms around the globe. It can soak, drench, saturate, moisten, sprinkle or shower. It is water. Capitalize on the texture of bathroom surfaces to either mirror water's gleaming smoothness or to be opposingly tactile and characterful. The choice is yours.

Open up your mind and think beyond the typical ceramic-tiled bath surround. Metals, stones, plastic, woods, glass and mosaic all have a place in the bathroom too. Despite a bathroom's usual small size, it's still possible to include many diverse textures within its four walls. Far from making the bathroom seem claustrophobic, artfully crafted textures flowing from floor to walls will open it up and bring a sense of spaciousness. A small room also gives you the chance to use materials that would be unaffordable in the quantities required elsewhere in the house. Used sparingly in a bathroom, they will lift it out of the ordinary and into the realm of sheer luxury.

bathroom
texture

opposite, below right: **This unassuming bathroom employs a combination of textures. Maplewood flooring is extended upwards to form the bath surround and a top to the low-level storage. Zinc sheeting provides the bath panel and cupboard doors. Six extra large marble tiles make a splashback.**

above: **Who said that brick cladding could never be tasteful? Oops, I think I did! Here, exterior rough stone, with light and shadow cast across its surface by overhead halogen lights, has been unexpectedly transported to a bathroom. Raw concrete, wax-polished to a light lustre, covers the floor and is repeated in the cast-concrete sunken bathing area decorated with white mosaic tiles for a swimming-pool feel.**

left: **A washbasin to die for. On one side of the understated waist-high marble room divider, a hand-crafted stone washbasin takes centre stage. The divider provides the location for the taps as well as incorporating shelves for towels and toiletry storage. This bathroom shows that stone can be seductive and sexy.**

waterfall
experience

It's official: the new stone age has arrived! You don't need to be an eccentric or in the cast of 'The Flintstones' to have cool concrete or seductive stone at home. This annexe to a master bedroom was an ideal location for an en suite shower room. But this was to be no ordinary conversion. The urban-caveman spirit was carried through using builders' basic materials – sandstone, concrete, glass and timber. The result was a fabulously luxurious wetroom.

This project was a large undertaking, which involved raising the floor to accommodate the plumbing and the underfloor heating – an essential bit of pampering. In addition, the ceiling was lowered to incorporate a super-efficient ventilation system and low-voltage halogen lights. Almost everything in the room was custom-made, from the curved glass screen to the concrete basin. It took a lot of careful planning to make sure that they all arrived on time.

right: **Wave-shaped opaque glass in front of the window gives privacy while allowing in lots of diffused light** (see page 169). **It also gives a traditional window a much more contemporary look.**

below: **A new central opening from the bedroom gives a complete view of the wetroom. The doors are made from maplewood with opaque glass inserts and they slide on visible industrial tracking. Their long, exaggerated handles echo the curved shapes in the rest of the room.**

the spirit
of the urban
caveman
is with us

space light colour texture detail

below: **The stainless steel toilet seat is of the type used in prisons – but with a wooden seat for comfort!**

above: **Neon lights are usually used outdoors, so there's no problem putting them in a damp environment like a bathroom. Here the dramatic manufactured qualities of the neon make a stunning contrast with the natural surfaces of the room.**

In order to keep a sense of unity in the room, it was decided not to have a shower tray. This meant that the floor in the wet area had to slope gently towards the drain. Shaking off sandstone's kerbside appeal by bringing it indoors, sandstone tiles were laid on the floor, and thinner ones were arranged in a wave pattern over part of the walls. The remaining wall space was rendered in rough concrete, its flawed, gritty, imperfect look achieved by dragging a piece of wood over the wet concrete.

The fundamentals of the wetroom were now in place, but it is the details that make it so spectacularly significant. Each of these was evaluated as if it were a work of art. For example, the light is sculpture first and light source second. Its intertwining strands of neon give it a real twist of ingenuity.

right: **A specially designed curved glass screen leaves plenty of room for a drenching waterfall experience. Thanks to the underfloor heating, the textured floor tiles make you feel as if you're standing on a warm, sandy beach.**

inset: **Texture is what the wetroom is all about, with natural and man-made materials cleverly juxtaposed.**

As this example shows, something as humble as a mirror can also become an object of desire. An unusual shape and Latin words associated with bathing were all that was needed to transform this mirror into a dramatic focal point.

5 steps to a brilliant bathroom

❶ Don't be rash – have a long hard look at your existing bathroom and analyse which elements work and which definitely need to be changed.

❷ Cost your project carefully. Get written quotations for all labour and materials from several contractors; and shop around at showrooms, superstores and builders' merchants to price fittings.

❸ Be imaginative with the space – the layout of your bathroom is of paramount importance, particularly if it is small. But even if you have a large room, you don't have to install a bath if you don't use one. Go for a super-deluxe shower instead.

❹ You needn't abandon style and luxury, but make sure you choose fixtures and fittings that are practical, durable and easy to care for.

❺ Above all, create a room for your needs, whether it incorporates a vanity unit for applying make-up or storage space for sports equipment.

drenching

The rest of the minimalist decoration adds to the interplay of materials. A wall-hung stainless-steel prison toilet adds its shiny hardness. A rubber vase and painted pebbles have a tactile quality. An under-stated robust plain birch table and, beneath it, smooth stones throwing attractive shadowy shapes across the floor bring a sense of organic nature.

At the end of the day, the difficulties involved in making the wetroom were well worth it. The result is an enviable textural experience, just right for washing away all your cares.

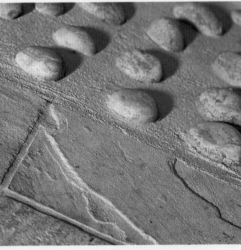

left: **Toning coloured pebbles were set into the concrete while it was still wet to give added texture.**

left and above: **In order for the washbasin to look like a mixing bowl sitting on a table, it was made from concrete by a specialist manufacturer. The mixer tap was wall-mounted and the plumbing disguised to keep the visual effect simple.**

nuggets + no-nos

● Be fearless: not every room in your home needs to meet with granny's approval.

● Warning! Don't attempt this project unless you have a large budget and skilled plumbers on hand.

The blueprint for a model bathroom lays equal emphasis on pleasure and practicality. So much for the ideal world. In reality, bathrooms do one thing: limit your layout options. We all have roughly the same sanitary fittings to squash in – bath or shower, washbasin and toilet. And all this has to go into what is often the smallest room in the home.

Getting the layout right first time is paramount. Not only is it inconvenient to move fittings around, it's also costly. But large bathrooms also have their layout problems. Here, the space needs to be compartmentalized so that it doesn't feel like a vast expanse with a couple of fittings dotted around the perimeter. Whatever size your bathroom, it's essential to allow for plenty of storage, so that all your bottles and lotions can be hidden from view. A combination of cupboards and open shelving usually fits the bill. Meticulous planning will ensure that you find space for everything – and that you don't lose out on style.

bathroom space

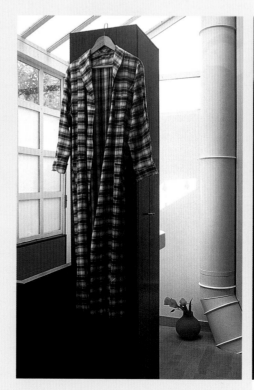

right and far right: **This minute bathroom is a miracle in a tight spot. The bath is sunk into the ground so that its outer edge is level with the wooden laminate floor. Sitting directly alongside is a slim 2m (6ft) high cupboard fitted with double doors for ease of access. Its far side supports the wall-hung basin.**

mosaic mad

Here's a bathroom that is cheerful, fashionable, hardwearing and achievable on a tight budget. The original floor linoleum was replaced by stylish tongue-and-groove flooring, laid widthways to make the room look wider. The turquoise woodstain really gives it the wow factor.

Using mosaic tiles all over the walls would have been very costly and this budget didn't stretch that far. Instead, walls painted in sunshine yellow, with a mosaic design gliding across, look every bit as glitzy. This design was repeated on the bath panel.

A large circular mirror had a hole cut in it to take an electric cable for a light and was hung above the washbasin. To finish it off, a border of contrasting copper-coloured mosaics was set around the edge.

Finally, as the window had clear glass, some privacy was needed. Full-length shutters with a bold graphic design turned the window into a prominent feature while shielding those inside from prying eyes during their relaxing and grooming sessions.

below left: **The glass mosaics of the bathroom are echoed in the imaginative accessories.** See page 163 for how to make a wall mosaic.

below right: **Tongued-and-grooved boards can be a sensible alternative if floorboards are in bad condition.** See page 158 for how to lay them.

inset: **Cutting a hole for the light fitting means you can justify having a larger mirror, which then means you can give it the glamour treatment!** See page 172 for how to make a Hollywood-style mirror.

space light colour texture detail

old bathroom
new tricks

Acrylic baths and walls clad diagonally in pine don't exactly shout out stylish glamour, so I didn't need much incentive to undertake a major revamp in this bathroom. The owners were traditionalists at heart, and didn't want anything too radical, so with this in mind, some more youthful colours were introduced, together with old-fashioned fixtures and fittings, but treated in a thoroughly modern way.

The floor was covered with unpretentious black and white floor tiles which are to a room what the little black dress is to the wardrobe – versatile and instantly glamorous. Fresh-looking pistachio and cheeky scarlet paint are the perfect complement.

This all goes to show that you can have an old-style bathroom and still be young at heart.

below right: **Reclaimed items such as this old radiator are much more characterful than modern ones. The scarlet paint effectively highlights its decoration.**

above left: **The walls were replastered to give them a grainy consistency, then pistachio-green paint was applied in a slightly shiny finish to exaggerate the flaws** (see page 163).

above right: **Last but not least, a stained-glass window was specially commissioned to reflect the classic styling of the room** (see page 169).

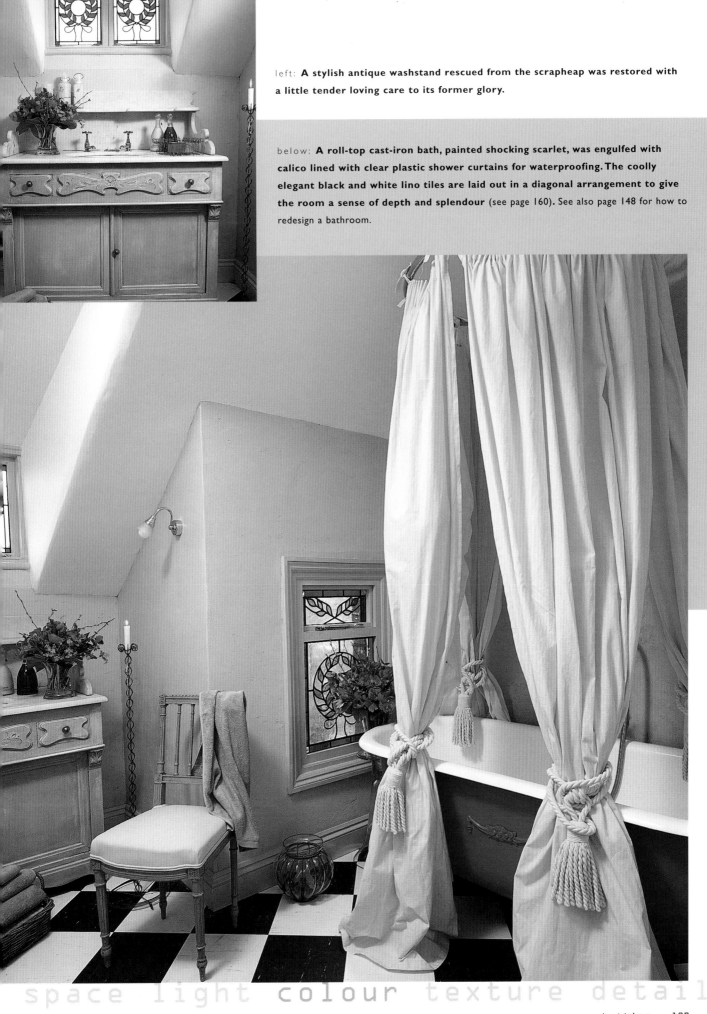

below: **A roll-top cast-iron bath, painted shocking scarlet, was engulfed with calico lined with clear plastic shower curtains for waterproofing. The coolly elegant black and white lino tiles are laid out in a diagonal arrangement to give the room a sense of depth and splendour** (see page 160). See also page 148 for how to redesign a bathroom.

space light colour texture detail

Sand, ash and fire: the essential ingredients that go to make that magical product – glass. I've

been fascinated by glass since childhood and am really excited by the artistic talent of the

people who work with it in its molten state. Glass offers myriad decorative possibilities

all around the home, but nowhere more than in the bathroom, where it can be used for

everything from vanitory tops and basins, to embellished shower screens and even floors.

bathroom glass

above: **A distinctive bathroom was created in a limited area with the help of space-defying glass. A custom-made glass panel acts as an unusual side wall for the bathtub.**

above right: **When your en suite bathroom looks this good, there's no point putting up solid barriers betweeen it and the bedroom. Instead, clear glass gives it a wonderful spatial feel.**

left: **Slabs of thick sandblasted glass work in an alluring way as bathroom countertops. A clear glass panel reveals the jewellery trays below, turning a practical feature into a thing of beauty.**

inset: **Glass bricks obscure a window, provide an easy-care splashback and act as a backdrop to a dazzling array of coloured glass.**

budget
makeover

Your bathroom looks like an embarrassing reminder of the 1980s...but you've only got a limited amount of money to spend. What do you do? Well, these two rooms – a shower room and a bathroom – show that the economically challenged don't have to suffer in silence. Even on a tight budget, you can still do a major renovation like this. With judicious use of paint, clever cost-cutting and lots of imagination, you can achieve something to be proud of.

Previously, this shower room was entirely covered in offensive red and white tiles, and the basin and shower had old-fashioned scarlet fittings. It would have been expensive to re-tile completely from scratch, but tiling straight over the existing wall tiles of the shower cubicle, and merely painting over the rest, saved the day. (Before you throw your hands up in horror, yes, you can tile on top of and paint onto tiles.) This left more money in the budget for good-quality finishing touches like the chrome taps and shower-head, a bathroom-themed clock, a wacky toilet seat and some unusual glittery flooring.

below: **Where in the world could you find a clock more suited to a bathroom than this one? Of course it's completely water- and steam-proof.**

nuggets + no-nos

● **Replace decaying shower cubicle doors with a humble shower curtain that will give you more elbow room.**

● **Being overlooked by neighbours is the fate of countless bathrooms. Use cut-outs of coloured self-adhesive vinyl on your windows for privacy.**

left: **Tiles don't have to go in straight lines. Instead you can mark out the wall with a kaleidoscope of abstract shapes and use a different colour in each shape** (see page 164). **As an alternative to a conventional blind, the window has been given a modern stained-glass effect using stick-on vinyl shapes** (see page 168).

below left: **The bathroom cabinet is made from a wooden picture frame with the cabinet built around it. The mirror was then glued to the back of the frame so the whole thing looks like a wall mirror. Chunky shelves provide more stylish space for toiletries** (see page 152).

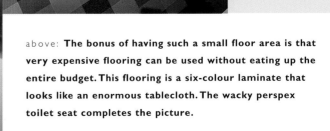

above: **The bonus of having such a small floor area is that very expensive flooring can be used without eating up the entire budget. This flooring is a six-colour laminate that looks like an enormous tablecloth. The wacky perspex toilet seat completes the picture.**

space light colour texture detail

Floral wallpaper and infinite shades of beige were more than the owners of this bathroom could handle. I decided to give them a glitzy Hollywood look, using some simple paint effects and a few sparkling accessories.

Since the budget didn't stretch to new wallpaper, I stripped off the old and painted over the plastered walls. The gilded paint effect helped to disguise the uneven surface. A simple frieze sprayed with gold paint livened up an otherwise dull bath, and gold-coloured taps to complement the colour scheme replaced the plastic ones. Finally, a mosaic mirror rounded off the million-dollar look.

below: **The faded lino definitely needed a facelift, so it was painted over in a rich mauve and some elegant swirls were added with a gold pen. Several coats of varnish help protect the design.**

above: **Glowing red and gold walls** (see page 165) **give the room a warm glow and create the perfect atmosphere for a long, candlelit bath.**

right: **Why settle for an ordinary square mirror when you can give yourself the star treatment?** See page 172 for how to make a Hollywood-style mirror.

above: **You don't have to spend a fortune to have a glamorous bathroom like this. A rich colour scheme of red, mauve and gold elevates it from the mundane to the magnificent.**

sleepi

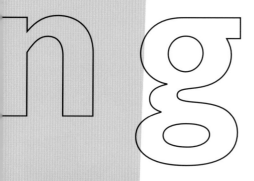

Think refuge. Now we lust after **comfort** in a **simple, sensuous space.** **Update** your bedroom by **ridding** it of **unnecessary fripperies.** Fussy, frilly sleeping areas belong to a **bygone era.**

n g

textured
tranquillity

Gravel, slate, concrete tiles and terracotta. Doesn't this sound like what you would need to build a patio? Well, could be, but surprisingly, when I integrated these ingredients with a TV, an immense seductive bed and two cats, I found the recipe for a tranquil, cocoon-like New-Age bedroom for myself. When I added a generous helping of fake suede and a good measure of fretwork, I had a show-stopping dressing room, too. If you're the sort of person who prefers shot-silk curtains and brocade bedspreads, then this unconventional decoration may not be for you, but keep an open mind.

Bedrooms are all about warmth and security, and what better way to satisfy those prehistoric instincts than with a fire? The chimney breast was opened up to accommodate this log-effect gas fire, which brings comfort at the flick of a switch and avoids messiness and smoky fumes.

below right: **The standard-sized bedroom door was replaced with an extra tall one to give a feel of extra security. One last-minute addition to the walls were triangles of red lycra stretched from floor to ceiling, to emphasize what a hot little number this bedroom is.**

below left: **An interesting feature in its own right by day, by night this unusual light casts a subdued glow.**

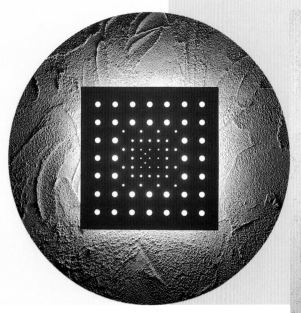

below: **Light plays an important part in creating the right atmosphere for a bedroom. Here, decorative light fittings are architectural features in their own right.** See page 170 for how to make an abstract light.

surrender to **your** prehistoric **instincts**

space light colour texture detail

nuggets + no-nos

● The horizontal lines of low-level storage are great if you want to avoid a room feeling overpowered.

● Bedroomy fabrics are not the only option. Think stripes, checks, fake suede, vinyl and rubber.

rough

above right: **The low-level units** (see page 153) **hide truck-loads of clutter but are totally unobtrusive. Lengths of rope nailed to the wall make an unusual alternative to a skirting board and complement the rough finish of the walls.**

opposite, right: **A place to put your feet up at the end of the day. A fireplace provides a welcome but unexpected focal point in a bedroom.**

The previously silky smooth walls were given a more primeval character with rough-rendered plaster. Their fussy extraneous details - architraves, skirtings and mouldings - just had to go. A palette of natural, understated colours continued the back-to-nature theme, while just a few accents of a robust red transform the room into a shrine to self-indulgence.

Toning low-level units beneath the fireplace provide the necessary storage for rarely used paperwork and favourite photograph albums. The top of the units, finished off with slate tiles and gravel, doubles as an exceptionally large hearth.

Now for the cosmetic details - the mascara and lipstick of the room! The bed was decorated with a tongue-in-cheek masculine feel. Hence the Prince of Wales check and the grey pinstripe covering the bed, both timeless classics, but dressed up with cushion covers in seventies-inspired cord, Aran knit and linen.

inset: **Get back to basics with an interplay of textures.** See page 163 for how to transform a wall with rendering and rope skirting.

5 steps to a fab bedroom

❶ **Evaluate your priorities. Try sleeping in your bedroom with nothing in it but a mattress for a few days to see what you really need and what you can do without.**

❷ **Let tranquillity prevail. Remove fussy architectural details and go for streamlined storage cupboards.**

❸ **Don't suffocate yourself with heavy drapes. Keep the room light and airy with sheer modern fabrics.**

❹ **If you need extra storage, place low shelving or a trunk at the foot of the bed for off-season linens or reading material.**

❺ **Soft pillows are a must for a great sleep. Buy the best you can afford plus an extra couple to prop yourself up with when you're reading in bed.**

right: **Putting the bed in the bay window frees up the rest of the floor space. The effect is softened by the backdrop of wooden venetian blinds with suede-effect curtains.**

below: **Mix the rough with the smooth for finishing touches like these cushions and pillows.**

To provide lots of storage for clothing, a spare
bedroom was invaded and turned into a posh-sounding
dressing room. This was filled with basic, inexpensive
wardrobes which, with a bit of imagination, were
transformed into something gloriously luxurious. A slim
space between one wardrobe and the door proved the
perfect spot for a shoe rack.

Privacy wasn't a problem thanks to sheets of opaque
glass fixed to the window frames. Plenty of daylight
floods in, but there's no need to worry about drawing
curtains or blinds when wandering about in the buff.

above left: **Paint, suede-effect fabric, fretwork panels and new handles are all that are needed to create spectacular wardrobes** (see page 153). See also page 154 for how to build a shoe rack.

above: **No space was wasted in the dressing room. The end-panels of the wardrobes are ideal for storing and displaying necklaces and scarves, while opaque glass in the windows offers much-needed privacy** (see page 169).

Bedrooms should feel pampering and soothing but if light is wrongly used your tranquillity will fall flat on its face. Remember that lighting isn't just about electricity. It encompasses daylight, candlelight and moonlight too. To get the right effect, your inner sanctum needs to be treated like a living room, with different styles and types of lighting for different activities, including those between the sheets! If it's evening and you're looking for an outfit in a drawer or wardrobe, you will need good overhead lighting, while if you've retired to bed to read a book, you want a bedside lamp. If you're indulging in a moment of passion, you won't want the room lit up like a lighthouse but will probably prefer soothing candlelight. For the morning after, glorious filtered daylight may be what you need.

This means that bedroom lighting has to be selected with care. Whatever choices you go for, make the lighting a triumph and avoid the mistake of lighting your bedroom as if an action scene from a James Bond film is about to be shot there!

bedroom light

far right: **Synthetic materials and applications are scorned in a converted attic room decorated in neutral tones and natural materials. The unadorned roof window allows unrestricted daylight to flood through.**

right: **This loft-style bedroom has two lighting needs well covered. Large windows let in natural light, while the headboard incorporates a pair of lights, thus negating the need for bedside lamps.**

understated
and streamlined

Soft squashy comfort and hard graphic shapes interact to make a refreshing bedroom where orderly storage is the priority. The owners dislike fussy frills and are very tidy by nature. Their brief was for inventive tailor-made storage, and plenty of it.

At first they veered towards a white colour palette, but decided that this would feel too austere and clinical. So white was fused with soft caramels, chestnut brown and the palest of lavender blues.

The three cupboards each with a niche-like recess for those 'need to grab in an instant' items are a talking point, but also conceal a wealth of shelving. Surprisingly, they are adapted from ready-made cupboards. For hanging storage, the couple opted to have a plain clothes-shop rail. The result is a room where everything is in its place yet still accessible!

below: **The bed occupies centre stage in this pared-down bedroom. The extra deep headboard incorporates housing for a ventilation duct and provides a handy resting place for family photographs, a pair of bedside lamps and an essential alarm clock.**

below right: **The chameleon-like headboard cleverly incorporates a roll-out storage unit for bedside reading and toiletries.**

below and right: **The doors of three shop-bought cupboards have been adapted to give them a custom-made look.** See page 127 for how to make a cupboard with cut-out cubes.

space light colour texture detail

Nothing looks more desperate than topsy-turviness in a room where tranquillity and calm should prevail. Bedrooms are never straightforward from the design point of view because they've always got to have mega storage capabilities. Ask any woman. You can never have enough wardrobes – somehow, miraculously, they'll always get filled!

Organized storage is the only way forward. Having piles of jumbled-up jumpers and odd shoes at the bottom of a wardrobe is not on. Personally, I can think of nothing more gratifying than opening a wardrobe and instantly putting my hand on the shirt I want. To achieve this level of organization, throw a critical eye over your jackets and trousers. To accommodate them, fit additional shelves, or add supplementary clothes rails so you can hang these shorter items from a lower rail. And if you are fortunate enough to have an unused adjoining room, why not turn it into a walk-in closet. Clothes-storage heaven.

bedroom storage

above: **Think beyond standard cupboards. The doors of this unconventional wardrobe have been made with wood faced with sheet metal. Hammer-finished galvanized steel and copper have been cut into an engaging wave pattern that is quite unique.**

right: **Ever thought that the displays in a boutique look appealing even if the clothes aren't that great? That's the secret of good display. Turning your own clothing and accessories into an exhibition rather than tucking them away behind doors is an inexpensive and attractive way of tackling a storage dilemma.**

right: **A provocative piece of furniture will add some oomph to
many a bland bedroom. A curious composition of drawers like
this one also offers loads of storage space.**

below: **This spartan warehouse bedroom solves its storage
predicament with a right-angled plywood screen fitted on one
side with a multitude of slim shelves, while hiding a clothes-
rail full of clothes from view on the other.**

purrfect
bedroom

What can you do when two people who live together have tastes that are poles apart? She likes old, traditional shapes and styles, while he's more of a groover. Now, I'm no marriage guidance counsellor, but other than have them go through an expensive divorce, my advice was to merge the opposing styles into an eclectic blend of the traditional - a pair of wardrobes and an iron bed - with a modern twist. The wardrobes were stained a rich mahogany colour, with the detail picked out in ebony-black. Chic chrome handles and silver leaf add an up-to-the-minute edge. Dressed with a white bedspread and blue fake fur throw, the bed has a new, refreshing image. The couple were thrilled with the result (and still together), while the neighbour's visiting cat was ecstatic!

below: **Plain wardrobes are updated with silver leaf** (see page 156) **placed randomly over the doors and bottom drawers.**

below: **This modern bed with a chrome-metal finish gives the traditional iron bed a new, refreshing image, especially when dressed with a blue fake-fur throw.**

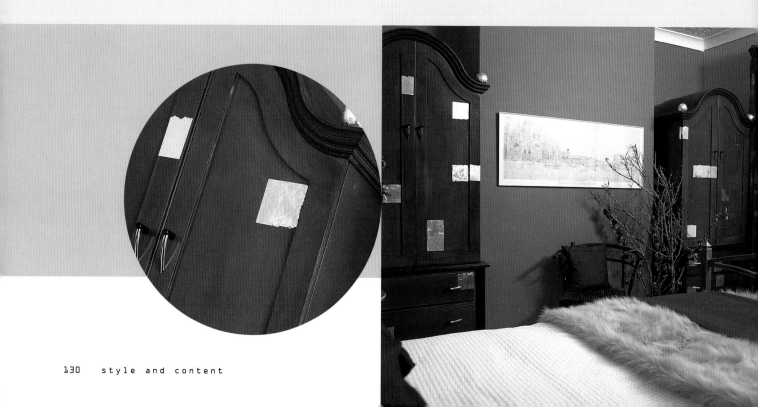

below: **A whimsical collage of words for love and passion in English, French, Italian, Irish and Finnish hangs directly over the bed – the perfect spot.**

space light colour texture detail

metropolitan loft

Is your loft full of unused sports equipment, dusty suitcases and Christmas decorations? Often neglected and abused, your roof space has the potential to become the extra room you've craved for - and even the best room in the house. The most common reason to convert a badly utilized roof space is an addition to the family. All too often, though, creative design and decoration get flung out of the window in the race against the midwife. But with a blank canvas like this, you have a golden opportunity to be daring. Move away from stereotypical boxy layouts and go with more radical fluid shapes and contrasting textures. Here, what could have been a very predictable attic conversion takes on the mood of a seriously smart sky-high metropolitan loft.

below left: **Unrestricted by conventional walls, daylight floods through the glass bricks into both the bedroom and the en suite shower room. A large circular mirror reflects more light and adds to the variety of textures.**

below centre: **Undulating wardrobe doors flow towards the curves of the en suite glass-brick bathroom wall.**

below right: **The brickwork along one wall lends an air of history without making the room too chintzy. And what better way to show off textural contrast than by overlaying smooth sheets of glass?**

be daring –
the sky's
the
limit

above: **The most exciting interiors are often created by looking at shapes, colours and materials with a fresh eye. Major projects such as this loft conversion, however, need careful planning. This conversion demonstrates how it is possible to keep a much-loved traditional Victorian bed and successfully place it in a modern context. Strategically placed pivot windows allow plenty of daylight into the room.**

space light colour texture detail

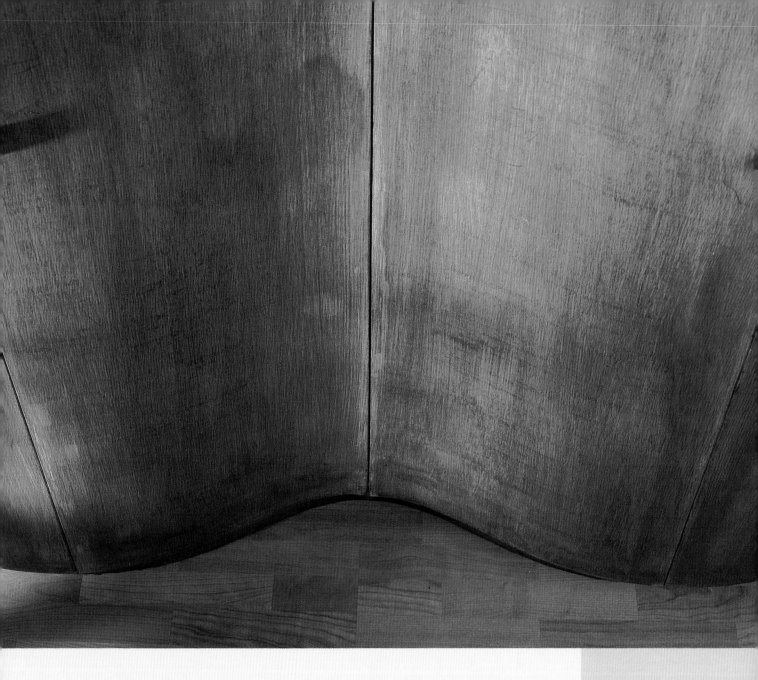

Unusually for a loft conversion, this one with its en
suite shower room was to become the master bedroom.
With two small children around the house, it was
important to make it Mum and Dad's very own oasis of
tranquillity, a place where they could recover at the
end of a long gruelling day. To achieve this, a calm,
uncluttered, controlled style was required. The
emphasis would be on the interplay of different
textures. Rough against smooth. All the furniture,
surfaces and decorative objects in the room had to
invite a tactile response. Every item had to do more
than just perform a function: it had to look and feel
fabulous as well.

above: **The wavy shape of
the wardrobe is the style
that flows through the whole
room.** See page 155 for how to
build a wavy wardrobe.

below: **Echoing the fluid shapes elsewhere in the room required a trip to the shops. This wonderfully wavy chest of drawers and superbly sculptural palette light are the perfect finishing touches.**

left: **Under-the-eaves storage is both ingenious and practical.** See page 151 for how to make a pull-out drawer.

flowing

To accommodate the need for lots of clothes storage, a spiced-up wardrobe was provided with doors with undulating curves made from bendy plywood. This changed the wardrobe from a merely practical item to an important architectural feature in its own right. From this would flow the entrance to the en suite shower room and the curved, glass-brick dividing wall.

It was important to be inventive with every bit of space. A wedge-shaped drawer on castors fitted under the eaves was the ideal use for this otherwise wasted area. Painted to match the walls, when closed it hides seamlessly away.

nuggets + no-nos

🖎 **Don't think square in a square room – put a bend in it.**

🖎 **A few well-made pieces of furniture and objects to treasure are better than lots of cheap items that will fall apart if you sneeze.**

5 steps for a fantastic fluid loft

❶ Don't be limited by straight walls. Think of them as something you can re-dress with fluid shapes and forms.

❷ Contrast rough textures such as brickwork with smooth zones of plaster, glass or wood.

❸ Let there be light! Elementary blinds are all the dressing that roof windows need.

❹ Normal wardrobes and chests are high on the lacklustre stakes. Adding a few waves makes any piece of furniture worth having.

❺ Throw a bit more cash than first planned at any en suite bathroom/shower room. It will make a world of difference to the choice of fittings that you can install.

below left: **Laminated wood flooring is in keeping with the smooth lines of the loft. Lights inset into the floor uplight the room's main features, in particular the curved glass-brick wall.**

below right: **A wall-hung toilet with hidden cistern leaves a small slate-tiled ledge for storage of toiletries.**

below: **Glass, chrome, slate and leopard print are the ultimate in textural contrast – a modern look that's full of surprises.**

below: **Since the loft was at the same level as the water tank, a pump was needed for the shower. Slate tiles covered the walls both inside and outside the shower cubicle so that an already small space was not divided up further visually.**

The en suite shower room would have been as rudimentary as possible if the owners had had their way. On my advice they went ahead with a more frivolous approach – good-quality chrome fittings rather than the original budget choices, and some gritty finishes for the surfaces. The luxurious glass washbasin looked magical when set against the variegated slate tiles, and was the definitive textural statement.

Unlike the more public rooms of a home, the bedroom often seems to take second place when it comes to decoration, and important details often get forgotten. These details are vital in any room, but in the bedroom they can add the finishing touches to your tranquillity.

As with any creative undertaking, designing a bedroom is a process that begins with an idea and evolves step by step into an intricately pieced jigsaw. Instead of looking at your room and wondering where to start, begin by taking a single source for your inspiration – for instance a favourite picture, piece of fabric or holiday memento – and then let this one item lead to all the rest. Once you have planned the big picture, the smaller features and details will fall into place and will prove as important as the overall scheme. Your finished bedroom will be a pleasure to wake up to.

bedroom detail

above: **The devil is in the detail. The dreaded bedside table is a necessary evil in practically all bedrooms. This well-constructed table top is an integral part of the headboard, but sitting snugly underneath is a pull-out cabinet on wheels which can slide back and forth.**

right: **A room full of naive charm pulls together large yet intricate details. The dominant charcoal-coloured textured bedhead is adorned with a mini gallery of prints. A blue resin stool becomes a handy bedside table, and a full-width trolley table glides across the bed for comfortable breakfasts.**

below: **A big cosy bed in an otherwise plain room has a heaped abundance of cushions and pillows in a multitude of colours. Natural daylight floods in across the highly lacquered floor from ingeniously placed low-level windows.**

how to achieve it

nuts & bolts

You've seen the designs – now it's time to make them. Many of those featured in this book are essentially simple projects that most people could copy as they stand, or adapt to suit their requirements. Several are projects that someone reasonably competent in DIY could do themselves, but some require the help of one or more professionals, be it electrician, specialist carpenter or plumber.

If you are attempting to do the projects yourself, you will benefit from the countless tips I pass on in this book. They are the result of my many years' experience in the interior design business and include some things I have learned through bitter experience! They are what makes this book so special. But, even if you are not planning to undertake the projects yourself, there is much more than just practical instruction here. You will also find guidance on the sort of things you will need to be aware of so that you can advance plan a project properly, and adequately instruct any professionals you have brought in to help you.

The symbols below will tell you which of the projects could reasonably be DIY jobs and those for which you will require some professional help.

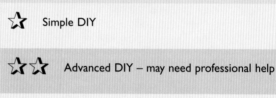

☆   Simple DIY

☆☆   Advanced DIY – may need professional help

☆☆☆   Professional help required

tool kit

Despite what many retailers will tell you, you don't need a truck-full of specialist tools for most simple decorating tasks around the home. But the following items, which are available from most DIY stores, are useful components of any tool kit.

Always try to keep your tools together in a box so that finding what you want is easy. Also, when you've finished painting, it's essential that you clean your brushes thoroughly so that when you come to re-use them, they are ready to go. Also, it's worth keeping a paint stain-removal liquid on hand – both for water-based and oil-based paint – for getting paint off furniture or carpets, just in case.

A selection of paintbrushes	Set square	Pencils and graph paper
Paint roller and tray	Spirit level	Scissors
Sponge	Hammer	Masking tape
Old cloths	Nail punch	Sandpaper/glasspaper
Brush cleaner	Steel tape measure	Sanding block
A selection of screwdrivers	Drill and bits	Adhesive to suit the job
A selection of screws and nails	Saw	Cutting tools to suit the job
Filling knife/spatula	Jigsaw	Disposable and heavy-duty gloves
Straightedge	Trimming knife	Face mask and goggles

electrical work

Unless you are 100% sure of what you are doing, you should always leave any electrical modifications to a qualified electrician. Check that they are approved by the National Inspection Council for Electrical Installation Contracting (NICEIC), a non-profit-making organization and the only one in the UK designed to protect consumers against unsafe electrical installations. Most importantly, the NICEIC will ensure that any faulty work carried out by any of its members is corrected at no cost to you. The Council (tel: 0171 564 2323) can supply you with a list of approved contractors, or you can find listings in your Yellow Pages or on the Internet at http://www.niceic.org.uk.

gas fitters

Any alterations involving gas must, by law, be undertaken only by an engineer registered with the Council of Registered Gas Installers (CORGI). These engineers carry a CORGI ID, so you can be sure you are getting the real thing. To find a registered installer in your area, call 01256 372300 and have your postcode to hand.

health matters

Many decorating materials are potentially dangerous so you should take sensible precautions when working with them. Always work in a well-ventilated room when using solvent-based paints, varnishes, glues and sprays. Protect yourself with clothing that covers exposed skin and with rubber gloves, and wear a mask over your mouth and nose. Use goggles to shield your eyes from dust and sprays and leave complex cutting with saws, knives or jigsaws to professionals. Make sure ladders are stable and always have at least a basic first aid box to hand in case of accidents.

There are particular warnings with regard to working with MDF (Medium Density Fibreboard). The dust produced – categorized as a softwood dust – when MDF is cut may cause skin disorders and asthma. For this reason, and because there have been other health concerns over formaldehyde emissions from MDF, it is vital that you open all windows and doors and protect your mouth and nose with a dust mask bearing the CE Mark EN149FFP2 when cutting it. Better still, leave it to a professional.

environmental concerns

In general, you should try to use materials throughout your home that cause the least amount of damage to the environment. Recycling is the key. Take unwanted furniture and other household goods to a charity shop or association for the homeless, and trawl such shops and salvage yards for items which you can customize. Economize on waste by using old cloths, rags and towels that can be re-used, rather than lots of disposable paper towels.

Solvent-based paints and varnishes contain damaging solvents that are very hazardous to the environment, so wherever possible, use water-based and acrylic ones instead. These will wash out of brushes and rollers with only water too – another plus point for the environment. Don't pour solvent-based products down the drain, as their harmful chemicals will infiltrate the water supply. Instead, take them to a recycling centre with solvent disposal facilities or contact your local authority to have them collected.

Timber is another problem area. Wherever possible use wood that comes from a well-managed, renewable source – look for the international FSC Trademark. And don't be tempted by mahogany, ebony, teak and African walnut, whose continued use threatens rainforests all over the world.

tiles

Tiling with ceramic tiles is a job that can be undertaken, with practice, even by the relatively inexperienced home decorator. However, fixing slate and sandstone tiles is a job for the professional tiler, as the tiles have to be cut using an angle grinder. Once fixed and grouted, these tiles should be sealed with a waterproof sealant, available from tile shops, if they are to be used in a damp environment. Since they are so porous, they need to be re-sealed at regular intervals. The following glossary will help you find your way through some common tiling terms:

tiles glossary

Cement-based tile adhesive Adhesive used for sticking ceramic floor tiles to wood, concrete and other materials.

Cement dye Pigment used to colour cement.

Grout Filler applied to the gaps between tiles.

Key Grooving or scratching a surface to provide a bond for tiles.

Latex Substance added to cement-based adhesive to give flexibility of movement when laying tiles on timber floors.

Mosaic tiles Small ceramic tiles available bonded together in sheets and strips by a layer of facing paper, which is soaked off with water after the tiles have been stuck in place.

Nibbling Cutting away small pieces of tile to get a precise shape.

Nippers Tool for nibbling tiles.

Ripple smalti Mosaics with gold or silver between two layers of glass.

Silicone sealant Adhesive used to stick tiles to glass and other surfaces.

Smalti Traditional mosaic tiles that are manufactured in Italy.

Vitreous glass tiles Opaque glass mosaic tiles with a bevelled underside to aid adhesion.

Water-resistant cement-based tile adhesive Specialist adhesive used externally for sticking tiles to metal or concrete.

glass

Glass is a wonderfully versatile substance, but many people are unaware of its true potential. There are many different types of glass and a number of associated processes and techniques – the following glossary will help you decipher the terms. For obvious reasons, glass needs to be handled with care, and the cutting and drilling of glass should always be left to a professional.

glass glossary

Acid-etching Glass decorating process.

Bevel Polished sloping surface around the edge of glass.

Casting Process of pouring glass in a mould.

Enamel Coloured substance used for painting glass.

Epoxy resin Adhesive commonly used to bond glass to glass or to other materials.

Firing Process carried out in a kiln to fix enamel to glass.

Float glass Ordinary window glass.

Frosting Light sandblasting.

Laminated Two layers of glass stuck together, usually with a clear plastic interlayer for strength.

Opaque Glass that is not transparent.

Resist Material used to protect areas of glass when sand-blasting or acid-etching.

Sandblasting Sand blown by compressed air to abrade the glass surface; results in semi-opaque glass.

Silicone sealant A common adhesive for bonding glass to glass or other materials.

Toughened glass Very strong safety glass, made by heating and rapidly cooling the glass sheet.

White acid Chemical used to produce a dense whitening of the glass.

acclimatizing materials

Porous materials such as cork absorb water and can swell, so it is advisable to leave them for at least 48 hours in the room in which they are to be used. Timber boards should be left for up to three weeks. That way, they will absorb any moisture in the atmosphere beforehand, instead of swelling and buckling afterwards. Similarly, vinyl tiles and sheeting expand with warmth and so should also be left to acclimatize in the room in which they are to be laid.

making a template

Some projects require that you make a template, whether it be to cut out a design from carpet or make a plywood shape for a worktop. Templates are best cut from fairly rigid paper (lining paper is ideal), card or plastic. Place the paper or card over the area in question and draw on your design to the correct size. If you are drawing freehand, work in pencil first in case you make a mistake, then when you are happy with your design, firm up the lines with a marker pen. If you are copying a shape or motif from another source such as a book, photocopy it at the size you want and stick it to the paper or card with spray adhesive. Then trace around the image with a marker pen. Using a scalpel or craft knife rather than scissors, cut firmly along your marked line in a flowing motion to ensure a smooth edge.

sanding floorboards

Sanding floorboards is a very noisy, messy and, potentially, dangerous job. Before you start, you should remove any furniture, curtains and furnishings. Seal doorways with plastic sheeting and open the windows. You will need to wear strong shoes, and goggles, earmuffs and a mask, and will have to hire a large sander and an edge sander, plus sheets of abrasive paper in different grades. You only have to pay for the sheets you use. To remove old paint or to level uneven boards, use a coarse paper first, followed by medium then fine. Use the edge sander in the same way for the edges where the large sander doesn't reach.

masking out

Many projects need you to paint certain areas while avoiding the adjacent ones. The simplest way to do this is to mask off the areas you don't want to paint use masking tape, which is sold in rolls like sticky tape but can be removed much more easily. Mark out the position of the area to be painted and firmly attach masking tape along its outside edges. Press down the edge of the masking tape to ensure that none of the paint will be able to seep underneath. Now you can paint right up to the edge without having to worry about smudges. Remove the tape when the paint is touch-dry and you should have a nice crisp edge.

There are many things to consider before undertaking any decorating project in the home. Budget is often a primary factor – and rightly so, because there is nothing more frustrating than spending more money than necessary. But before you part with any cash, take a good look at your room and decide if you could get away with just a facelift: a lick of paint here, new curtains or blinds, a few new features there. Removing old architectural features can also help update the look of a room. All of this can be done inexpensively and, if you have the time, you may be able to do it yourself.

For anything more major, you'll probably need to bring in the professionals. Personal recommendation or seeing previous work is often a good way of choosing workmen, but taking a look in the back of their van can also be very revealing. If it's dirty and untidy, chances are their work will be messy and they'll leave your house in a state, too.

Always get written quotations from several different contractors, taking care to ensure that they are comparable. The quotations can help you determine how much you will need to spend. You may decide that you could spend more if you staggered the cost, but bear in mind that this will be more disruptive. Workmen often require money upfront to purchase materials, so make sure that you can provide this, and be sure to have a written contract before you hand over any money. Don't forget that major refits often involve many different tradespeople and can be an organizational nightmare. A hired professional can help with the co-ordination.

Whatever you decide and whoever you involve, persevere to make sure your revamp is something you want, not something that is most convenient for your builder. The following checklists for different activities in the home will help you focus your aims and requirements so that you end up with the best results.

living and integrating checklist

Does your space fulfil your needs?

Would you like more space? Can this be created by adding an extension, or by knocking through into an adjacent room?

Would removing or blocking up any doors give more space and flexibility?

Is there enough storage space? Do you need more, or do you just need to be creative with what you have?

Do you need an area that can double up as a space for overnight guests?

Do you need everything that is in the room or can you get rid of things for a more uncluttered feel?

What flooring best suits your needs – something for warmth or comfort, or something that is easy to keep clean?

If you are thinking of wooden flooring, will you need underfloor insulation to reduce noise and cut down on draughts?

If you are considering a coir or seagrass floor covering, will it be comfortable for bare feet or for your crawling children?

Is there enough natural light? Would removing curtains help?

Would your windows look more up-to-the-minute with roman or venetian blinds?

What effect would you like the lighting to make – bright and welcoming, or gentle and relaxing?

Do you need task lighting for reading and working?

Does furniture need to be dumped or just given a facelift?

Would you gain space with mobile room dividers?

Have you got enough height to create a mezzanine level?

Would the addition of a platform in a bedroom or dining area give you useful additional space below the platform?

With any multi-functional room, make a decision about which function takes priority and give it preference.

Are there any rooms which are seldom used while others

leap

are over-used? Can you strike a new balance?

If you work from home, use a room or area within a room that won't dominate your home life.

If your budget is minuscule you can still integrate spaces successfully. Something as simple as a portable fabric screen will allow two activities in one room.

If your home is compartmentalized but integrating sounds right for you, just do it. Integrating can make your home feel twice the size that it actually is.

Think laterally when integrating. Space can be carved out both vertically and horizontally in practically every home.

eating checklist

Can you work with your existing kitchen layout to avoid the cost of moving plumbing and power supplies?

Are the services – plumbing, electrics, ventilation – in good working order, or do they need to be replaced?

Are the work surfaces at the correct height for you?

Do you need more light, especially over work surfaces and eating areas?

Do you have enough power points?

Are your existing appliances in good condition, energy-efficient and easy to clean, or do you need to buy new ones?

Is the present flooring practical?

Do you need more storage or food-preparation space?

Do you want to be able to eat in the kitchen?

Do you need a phone in the kitchen and perhaps a small office area if you do not have one elsewhere in the house?

Do you need space to incorporate laundry facilities, or is there room for that elsewhere?

Do you need to have a freezer in the kitchen, or can that stand somewhere else and still be accessible?

Do you need to make room for a microwave?

bathing checklist

Is your bathroom big enough for comfort? Can you gain space by breaking into an adjoining room or hallway?

Does the door open inwards, taking away valuable space? If so, could it be hung the other way?

Does a shower door open into the room? Could it be made to hinge the other way?

Is the plumbing satisfactory, or does it need an overhaul?

Do you need a pump to make a shower more powerful?

Is the bath big enough?

Do you have enough elbow room in the shower?

Is the basin the right height? Do you need more than one?

Is there adequate lighting, heating and ventilation?

Is the flooring serviceable and attractive?

Do you need a shaver socket?

Is the existing layout efficient?

Is there enough storage space? Do you need more, or do you just need to be creative with what you have?

Do you need space to exercise?

Do you need somewhere to apply make-up?

sleeping checklist

Can you create additional storage under your bed with pull-out drawers or bags for out-of-season clothes or bedding?

Is the position of your bed maximizing the floor space?

Would wall-mounted lamps save bedside-table space?

Do your wardrobes need to be ripped out or would new doors and a splash of paint spruce them up?

Do you have enough space to create a laundry cupboard with ironing board and hanging rails?

Can you see the TV and reach the telephone from the bed?

Would something as simple as buying new bed linen waken up the room?

how to
room planning

...redesign a bathroom ☆☆☆

You move into a new home and everything's great, except the bathroom. You can't use the toilet without feeling you're about to fall into the bath, you want a shower and there isn't one, and there's a lot of wasted space around the washbasin. Sometimes you just wish you could rip the whole lot out and start again. Well, you can – within reason.

The main restriction in any new design is the location of the toilet. The maximum distance between a toilet and the soil stack into which it discharges is governed by the Building Regulations and by the need for the waste pipe to be installed with enough fall for the disposal of the waste. If you want to locate a toilet further away than the 6m (20ft) maximum permitted, then you must fit a macerator unit which breaks down the waste by means of an electric motor and pumps it to the soil stack.

Something else to bear in mind if you are planning to move a toilet is that a toilet waste pipe is about three times the diameter of waste water pipes from a bath, shower or sink, so it will need more underfloor space. Often, the easiest and best-looking solution is to raise the whole bathroom floor to accommodate the new plumbing rather than have an ugly boxed-in section. By doing this, you can have everything in your bathroom exactly where you want. Remember though that a raised floor will restrict ceiling height above it and may require a step up into the room from outside.

A well laid out bathroom is one with enough space around each sanitary fitting so that you can use it comfortably. Problems usually arise only in very small bathrooms, where these activity spaces have to overlap. A bathroom should also make the best use of the light source while still maintaining the crucial element of privacy. My plans (see diagram) show before and after layouts of the bathroom featured on page 108. Originally, the toilet was located by a low window, so it lacked privacy and also obscured an important light source. The double basins (one of which was rarely used) were positioned so that the users were facing away from the light source, casting their faces in shadow. And the radiator was tucked around a corner, so that only a part of the room felt the real benefit of its heat. Switching the positions of all the fixtures and dispensing with the extra basin not only made the bathroom more practical but made it feel more spacious, too.

before

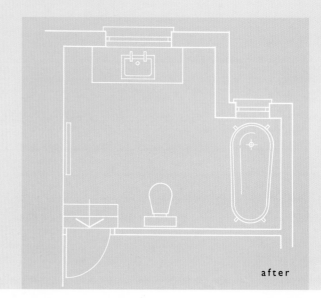

after

page 108   page 16

...knock rooms into **ONE** ☆☆☆

This is a project that requires a lot of planning. The first step is discuss your plans with your local authority to see if they comply with building and planning regulations. Then you will be aware of any legal constraints from the start. The work must be planned by a qualified architect or structural engineer and carried out by professional builders, and before starting you must notify your local authority building control department so they can inspect the work in progress.

Also bear in mind that removing supporting walls from a room can seriously weaken the structure of the building unless some other means of support is provided. This usually means spanning the room with beams called rolled steel joists (RSJs). In the example below, more space was also created by adding an extension to house the kitchen.

When the work is complete you will have a vast open space to play with. However, it is a good idea to break up these large expanses in an informal way with sofas, tables or large floor-standing urns and vases. Keep these defining structures low in order to allow the light to flood in unimpeded through the windows. The space will work best if you assign different functions to different areas. Locate the dining area close to the kitchen so that food does not have to be carried the length of the room in order to be served. Create a cocoon of comfort around a fire with comfy furniture. Think large-scale when it comes to the furniture, rugs and pictures, but don't place sofas and chairs too far apart or you'll end up having to shout across the room. The feeling of open space will make it the most relaxing place in the house and you'll soon realize that taking down the walls was your best idea ever!

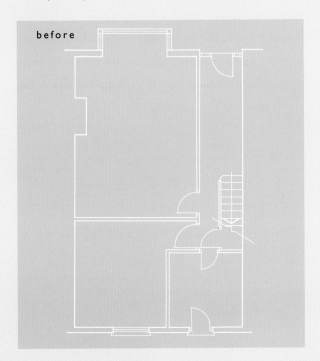

before

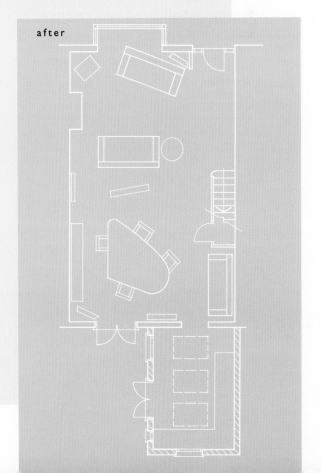

after

page 50

...draw up a **kitchen plan** ☆☆☆

Drawing up a properly scaled floor plan is invaluable when changing the layout of most rooms in the home, but nowhere more so than the kitchen. While kitchen showrooms have the facility to make plans for you, they may be designed to suit the existing positions of the plumbing and electricity, which will limit the design. You need to start a stage earlier by really thinking about how you want your kitchen to work, in order to find out if the location of power and water supplies needs to be changed.

Make a rough sketch of your kitchen area, including the position of windows, doors, radiators, power points and so on. Don't forget to indicate whether a door opens into or out of the room, as this will make a lot of difference to the available floor space. Now measure the length of walls, width of doors, distances between power points, and mark the measurements on your sketch.

Decide on a scale – for instance 1m/1ft to a square – and redraw your sketch onto an appropriate size of graph paper. The larger the scale the more accurate you can be.

Using a pencil, sketch in several different layouts – not forgetting to include any furniture you want, such as tables and chairs – until you find one that works best for you. Ask yourself whether your kitchen is to be strictly for food preparation or whether you want a more social room where people sit and kids do their homework. Allow for all the different activies: food preparation and cooking, eating, cleaning and recycling, and storage.

If you do want to change the position of the electricity and water sources, get an electrician and plumber to come to your home and explain your proposed layout to them. They will be able to tell you whether your scheme is feasible or not, and will be able to give you an estimate of how costly it will be.

Now's the time to go to the showroom. They may be able to reproduce your plans and supply a three-dimensional drawing of your proposed kitchen so that you can see what it will actually look like. Alternatively, you can call in a specialist kitchen company who will come to your house and, working from your plans, will re-measure your kitchen and draw up their own set of plans.

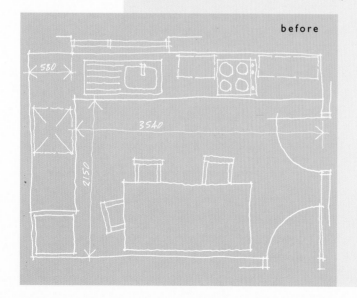

before

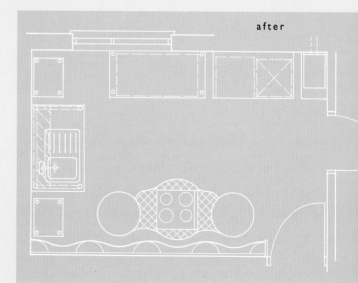

after

how to
storage

page 135   page 72

...make a **pull-out**
drawer ☆☆☆

If you think the area under the eaves is a waste of space, then think again. With careful planning it can be made to work for you. This pull-out unit made of plywood and MDF makes the most of that space. You can discuss with your builder the best place for the drawer and you'll need to get a carpenter to help you. The unit slides into a hole cut in the wall, so that when it is closed, it lies flush. The sides of the unit slope downwards from the front, mimicking the pitch of the roof and allowing the unit to fit snugly into the space (see diagram). Castors enable it to be pulled out completely for good access. Add a wooden surround and paint the front the same colour as your wall for a seamless finish.

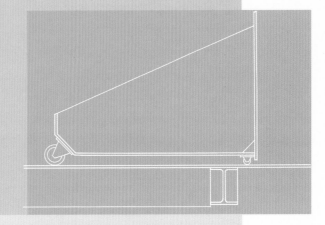

...design a **clever**
corner unit ☆☆☆

Blow away the cobwebs from a neglected corner with this unusual storage cupboard. This corner unit of painted and varnished MDF or plywood both conceals all electronic gadgetry and gives a room an interesting focal point. The central section houses the TV and video, and has a door which slides back into the unit giving an unobstructed view of the TV from anywhere in the room. Other sections hold the CD player, speakers, CDs and video tapes. The doors of these sections have push catches for a smooth-fronted finish.

To plan a unit like this, you must first decide what it has to contain and how much of your corner is to be taken up by it. Measure the size of your TV and music system so you can allocate enough space for them. Don't forget to allow for shelves for your CD and video tape collection. These can be built to the exact height, depth and width required to maximize your storage space. Think about where the power is to come from so that all the holes you will need for cables can be included as the unit is being built. Finally, give your drawings and measurements to a good carpenter to bring it all to life and build it into your corner.

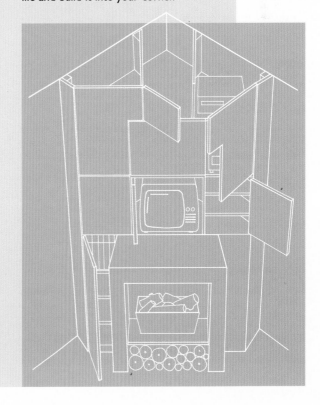

page 113   page 80   page 40, 41   page 120

...make **deep** shelves ☆☆

A stack of deep shelves looks so much more stylish and solid than narrow ones, particularly when they are hung so the fixtures are invisible. First, measure the distance from wall to wall to give you the length of each shelf. Next, measure the depth from front to back and cut two pieces to these dimensions from a sheet of 6mm (¼in) plywood or MDF. These will be the top and bottom surfaces of the shelf. Cut two battens from 50 x 50mm (2 x 2in) timber to fit on either end of the space, and fix them to the walls with screws and wallplugs, making sure that they are level by using a spirit level. If you want the shelves to be chunkier than 50mm (2in), you will need to fix a separate set of battens to support the lower part of the shelf.

Screw one piece of the plywood or MDF in place on top of the battens, and the other underneath. Cut a piece of 6mm (¼in) board 60mm (2½in) deep – or deeper if your shelf is chunkier – and to the same length as the shelf. Pin and glue this in place across the front of the shelf. Countersink all holes so they can be filled, sanded and painted over.

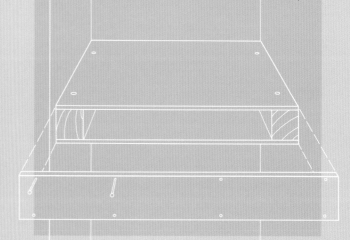

...make **cardboard tube** storage ☆

Bees know best when it comes to making the most of the available space. They build up their honeycombs so not a single nook or cranny is wasted. Take a leaf out of their book with this cardboard-tube storage idea. It fits so neatly into an alcove and is so great for storing small things like CDs, you could be forgiven for thinking that alcoves were designed with just this in mind. Buy your tubes from a company specializing in industrial packaging (see stockists).

To work out how many tubes you need, measure the width of the alcove and decide to what height you want to fill it. Divide the width by the diameter of one tube to see how many tubes you'll need for each row. Divide the height in the same way to see how many rows you need. If necessary, cut the tubes to length. Colourwash them to match the walls and coat them with acrylic varnish to protect them. All you have to do now is stack the tubes in the alcove. They will sit securely in place without needing to be attached to each other.

page 123

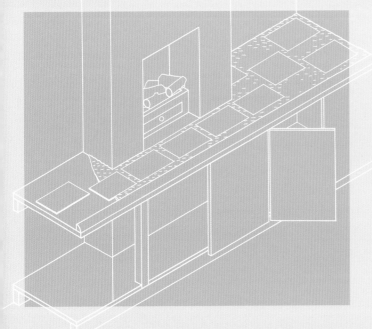

...make **low-level**
storage ☆☆☆

Low-level storage is much less obtrusive than the upright sort. Get a carpenter to construct a wooden frame of 50 x 50mm (2 x 2in) timber running from wall to wall. If it surrounds a functional fireplace, the adpacent parts should be made from non-combustible material to comply with the Building Regulations. The top is covered with 9mm (⅜in) plywood, and doors made from 6mm (¼in) MDF are attached to the front. Fit the doors with push-catches and pin and glue 30mm (1¼in) quadrant moulding to the top front edge of the unit to form a lip. Behind this, fit a row of slate tiles with white spar gravel in between.

...**transform** ready-made
wardrobes ☆☆☆

Plain wardrobes or cupboards can be turned into real dazzlers with the help of fretwork panels. Design inspiration came from fabric, but you could use anything you like as the inspiration for yours – an abstract shape or an architectural detail. Measure the size of the panels you will require and take the measurements, together with a sketch of your idea, to a company specializing in fretwork. Ask them to show you a drawing of how the finished panels will look for your approval, or, if possible, a computer-generated drawing. Have them make the panels out of 6mm (¼in) MDF and supply them ready-primed.

While the panels are being made, prepare the rest of the wardrobe. Prime the end panels, the door frames and the edges of the doors (there's no need to paint the door faces as they will be covered with fabric) using an acrylic primer.

When this is dry, apply one coat of matt emulsion paint, and when that is dry, apply two coats of matt acrylic varnish.

Cut lengths of suede-effect fabric to the same dimensions as the panels, then spray the wardrobe doors with extra-strong aerosol adhesive. Fit the fabric in place and smooth it down carefully with the palm of your hand. Spray-paint the fretwork panels using a water-based aerosol paint. This is a labour-intensive job as you need to spray each panel from several angles to ensure that all the fretwork is covered. It is a job that is best done out of doors on a still day. Finally, use panel pins to attach the fretwork panels to the doors on top of the fabric.

page 123   page 19

...build a **shoe rack** ☆

Storing shoes is always a problem – too often they end up in a jumble at the bottom of your wardrobe. For a streamlined storage solution, you could make a display rack for your footwear, using up a spare alcove. If you want to make full use of the available wall space between a wardrobe and a wall, do as I did, and attach a floor-to-ceiling panel to the end of the wardrobe and to the wall, and attach the shoe racks to these.

Start by cutting pairs of 19mm (¾in) diameter chrome hanging rails to length to fit between the wardrobe and the wall. Starting at the bottom, screw one 19mm (¾in) end bracket to the wall and slide the rail into the bracket. Now slide another bracket onto the other end of the rail. Using a spirit level to ensure that it is level, attach the loose bracket to the opposite side panel and screw it in. You now have your first bottom rail in position.

Resting the toe of one shoe on this rail, use the position of the heel to locate the lowest rear rail about 100mm (4in) above the front one. The heel of a high-heeled shoe should hook over the rear rail, with its toe resting on the front one. Mark the location of the rear rail on the two side panels, use a spirit level to ensure that these two points are level and fit the rear rail in the same way as the first one.

Draw two vertical lines up the sides of the alcove, using the positions of the front and rear rails you have just fixed as starting points. Make pencil marks at 200mm (8in) intervals along each of the four lines. Use these marks to locate the remaining brackets, then fit all the remaining rails.

...make a **revolving TV box** ☆☆

Turned off by your TV set? Well, this useful revolving box will disguise a TV and video and also give you somewhere to keep the remote control and video cassettes. Make a box from 12mm (½in) MDF large enough to accommodate your TV and video and to fit shelves inside for them. Drill a hole in the base of the box wide enough to take the power and aerial cables of your equipment. Now cut a square base to the same width and depth of the box, with a slot for the power and aerial cables. Screw the box and base panel to a turntable. Feed the cables through the centre hole of the turntable and the box and adjust so they feed around the edge. Attach a door fitted with a push catch. Decorate the box by sticking pictures to its sides with aerosol adhesive. Protect them with two coats of clear acrylic varnish.

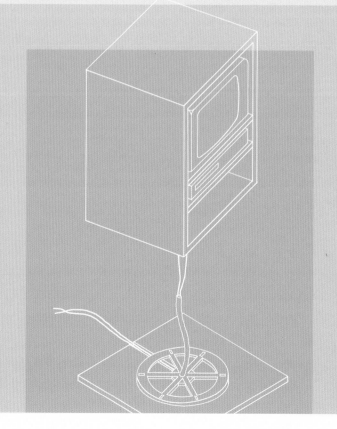

page 134

...build a **wavy wardrobe** ☆☆☆

Standard wardrobes get the wave treatment with this novel adaptation. Have a carpenter build a wardrobe carcase to your desired specifications. Draw a wavy line on the floor in front of its base (a piece of hosepipe gives a good firm line from which to trace a curve) and get the carpenter to build a plinth along the line. Now make a paper template of the shape of the plinth, and have your carpenter build two curved formers (one for each pair of doors) from plywood profiles and 50 x 25 mm (2 x 1in) battens to the same shape (see diagram 1). These will be used as moulds for the doors.

Clamp a sheet of 6mm (¼in) flexi-plywood to each of the formers (see diagram 2) and brush woodworking adhesive onto their surface. Partially release the clamps and stick a second sheet to each curved surface, and clamp them firmly again. When the adhesive has formed an initial bond, repeat with a third piece of plywood to make two curved laminated sheets 18mm (¾in) thick. Leave the assemblies to set.

Remove the curved sheets from the formers and get your carpenter to use them to cut four doors to size and to fit them to the wardrobe carcase so that they butt neatly against the curved plinth. Finally lay a piece of plywood on top of each wardrobe and mark the curve of the doors on them. Cut along the curved lines and fit the pieces to the tops of the wardrobes so the doors close neatly against them and keep dust out of the wardrobes. Finally, stain the plywood exterior with a woodstain and coat with acrylic matt varnish to finish.

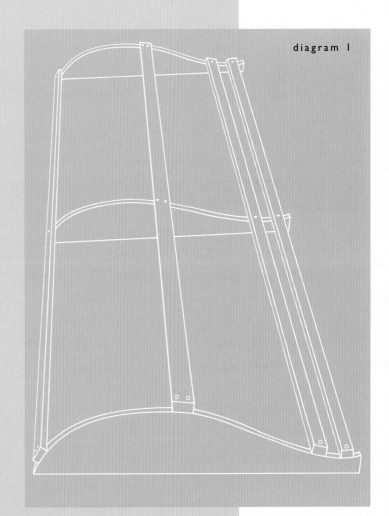

diagram 1

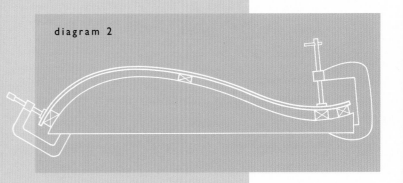

diagram 2

page 50   page 130

...build a **scaffolding wash station** ☆☆☆

A scaffolding structure built for your sink adds a funky look to your kitchen, but could easily be adapted for storage shelves for other areas in your home. Aluminium scaffold poles are very inexpensive and have a dull silver finish which doesn't need to be painted or varnished.

Measure the area to be covered by the structure and have your poles cut to size. Bolt the structure together using normal scaffolding brackets (see right). Stick a perforated alumimium sheet to the wall and cover the bottom part with a sheet of polypropylene to act as a splashback (see above).

To find the width of the worktop, measure the gap between the upright poles. Then add about 30cm (12in) to this figure. This allows 10cm (4in) on either side for an overhang to cover the horizontal poles which support the worktop. Have the worktop cut to size. To secure the worktop firmly, mark on its front and back edges where it touches the four upright poles, then drill four holes and plug with four dowels at this point. Drill a hole into each upright scaffolding pole at the point where it meets the worktop. Now slacken off the front scaffolding brackets and extend the gap between the front and back of the entire structure so there is enough room for the worksurface with its dowels to be slipped into place. First fit the two rear dowels into the holes on the rear upright poles. Then push the dowels in the front of the worksurface into the holes in the front two upright poles. Apply pressure to the front of the structure as you carefully re-tighten the brackets.

Get a plumber to fit the sink into the worktop and plumb it in. Additional shelving can be made from standard scaffolding planks placed straight onto the horizontal poles. To complete the industrial look, edge them with angle bead – the metal bead normally used by plasterers to form corners on walls that are about to be plastered.

...**update** a traditional **wardrobe with silver leaf** ☆

Silver leaf is not something you would normally see on a wardrobe, but it brings old-fashioned styles bang up to date. Although delicate, sheets of silver leaf are fairly easy to work with. First lay newspaper in front of the wardrobes to protect the floor. Working in a well-ventilated room, take a book of silver leaf and spray the individual leaves still attached to their backing paper with aerosol adhesive. Position the silver leaf on the wardrobes and peel off the backing paper. Silver leaf is very fragile, so protect it with clear acrylic varnish, spraying it on rather than brushing it on.

page 127   page 26

...make a cupboard with **cut-out cubes** ☆☆

Ever forgotten which cupboard you've put things in? This clever adaptation of a ready-made cupboard allows a handy display of their contents. The central shelves and vertical dividers within the wardrobe carcase form the storage cube that will be exposed by the cut-outs in the doors. You can vary the size of the cube to suit the scale of the wardrobes, but this one is 400mm (16in) square.

Find the centre point of the shelves and mark points 200mm (8mm) to either side to indicate where the vertical dividers will be fixed. Cut the dividers to size from 19mm (¾in) MDF and fix them in place, driving nails down through the upper shelf and up through the lower one.

Close one of the doors and reach inside the cupboard so you can mark the position of the divider on the inner face of the closed door. Repeat the process to mark the other door. Then take the doors off and cut out the marked sections with a jigsaw. Sand the cut edges, replace the doors and voilà! You now have easy access to all those easy-to-lose items.

...make **cool** **hi-fi** storage ☆☆

If you don't want the hassle of making a cupboard but want to hide away your techno equipment, why not improvise? This fireplace opening, which had already been fitted with shelving, only needed a set of doors across the front to become a home for hi-fi. The doors give access to the music system and the shelves and, with their geometric cut-outs, are a great focal point for the room.

To make the doors, cut a sheet of 9mm (⅜in) plywood large enough to cover the front of the shelving and to the height you want. I made these doors taller than ordinary doors to give the room a different perspective. Then mark the positions for the cut-out shapes onto the plywood by measuring the location of the hi-fi, books and so on on the shelves. Cut out the shapes using a jigsaw. Now cut the sheet in two to form the two doors. Paint the front in matt emul-sion and use a contrasting colour for the exposed edges of the cut-out shapes. Finally, hang the doors on slim vertical wall battens, stand back and admire!

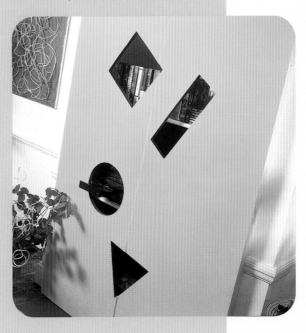

page 61

page 106

...paint a **kitsch kitchen** floor ☆

Feeling a little crazy? Then this floor is just right for you. First lay cork tiles over the entire floor (see page 160). Cork absorbs paint better than other floor surfaces, but lino or floorboards can also be painted. After the adhesive has dried, use a roller to apply a coat of acrylic primer. When dry, paint with a coat of lilac emulsion (you can, of course, choose a different colour if you wish). To create the circles, you'll need to get out some of your not-so-finest crockery. Place a few plates, mugs and egg cups randomly on the floor. When you're happy with the layout, draw around the edge of each with a pencil. Remove all the dishes, and paint the circles in different shades of emulsion paint. I used yellow, blue and jade. When these have dried, add a few overlapping circles for more interest. Finally, protect the floor with four or five coats of quick-drying acrylic floor varnish. When the floor is dry, grab a partner for a quick jive.

...lay and stain a **tongued-and-grooved** floor ☆☆

If your floorboards are in poor condition, why not lay new tongued-and-grooved boards on top instead of spending time trying to improve them? Before starting, leave the boards for up to three weeks in the room where they are to be laid to acclimatize (see page 145). This will ensure that they don't bow after the floor has been laid.

Lay the first row of boards along one wall, with the grooved edge against the skirting board facing the wall. Fix them to the existing floor by driving lost-head nails through the tongues at an angle of about 45 degrees, making sure that the nail does not protrude below the tongue. Use a nail punch when the nail head gets close to the board. Fit the grooved edges of the next row of boards over the tongues on the first row. The first nail heads will now be hidden from view; this is called 'secret nailing'. Continue across the floor, butting the boards together and secret-nailing them in place.

When the whole floor is finished, lightly sand the board surface with a power sander (see page 145) and vacuum up the dust. Following the manufacturer's instructions, apply a tinted varnish, brushing it along the planks in the direction of the grain. The more coats of varnish you apply, the darker the colour will become. Because it incorporates a stain, using a ready-tinted varnish will minimize the time that your room is out of action.

page 34   page 24

...lay reclaimed
floorboards ☆☆☆

If you yearn to find lovely old floorboards under your carpet, but all you find when you peel it back are slabs of bare concrete or sheets of hideous chipboard, don't despair: you can bring a manor-house-floor to your home with a trip to your local salvage yard. Old floorboards are easy to come by and relatively inexpensive. Have your room measurements with you when you go looking, as you'll need to buy enough boards for your needs. They could all have been sold by the

time you return for some more. You also need to decide which direction you want your floorboards to run across the room. One way may be more economical than another. The people at the salvage yard should be able to advise you. In order to lay the boards on a concrete floor, you need to fit battens across the floor at right angles to the direction of the boards and around the edges of the room (see diagram). Laying the floor itself is a job best left to a professional.

Once laid, the floor will need to be sanded (see page 145) as the boards will probably all be of slightly different thicknesses. Start with a large sander fitted with a coarse sheet of abrasive, and sand diagonally in one direction, then diagonally in the opposite direction, before finishing off by sanding in the direction of the grain of the boards. This gives the best results on uneven boards.

Next, use the edge sander for the areas the large sander could not reach, first fitted with coarse abrasive, then with the medium and lastly with the fine grade. To finish off the floor, use the large sander again, but this time working only in the direction of the grain of the wood. Use medium abrasive first, then finish off with the fine grade. Be careful not to sand all the character out of the boards. Vacuum up any dust.

Finally, your newly sanded floor needs some protection. Varnishing gives a long-term protective finish, but wax looks more natural and feeds the wood, too. However, wax needs re-applying frequently, so it is not such a good choice if your floor is to get a lot of wear and tear.

...match new
floorboards to old ☆

So you're tired of the old carpet and decide to have lovely shiny floorboards instead. You take up the carpet, and there in all its glory is the original floor...with several replacement timbers looking a lot lighter than the originals. Disaster? Well no, not really. The first thing to do is to sand the boards with a sander (see page 145), and vacuum up the dust. Then get a colour swatch of woodstains and choose the one that most looks like the original floorboards. Buy the smallest available tin just to try out the colour. Practise on a very small area, in a corner near the wall or skirting board if possible. It may take several colour samples to get an exact match. Once you're happy with the shade, stain the newer boards to match the older ones. When the woodstain is dry, give the whole floor several coats of acrylic varnish.

page 94   page 108

...lay **cork, vinyl** or **lino** tiles ☆☆

Floor tiles can lend a room instant glamour and are relatively simple to lay. First lay hardboard over existing floorboards to give a level surface, pinning the sheets down along the edges and across the centre at 150mm (6in) intervals. Then apply a mixture of water and PVA glue to the hardboard to act as a primer. This will improve the adhesion between the hardboard and the tiles. Allow it to dry completely. Place the tiles in the room so that they acclimatize (see page 145).

To get a neat, even border and cope with walls that are seldom perfectly square, you need to find the centre of the floor and work outwards from there. If you want to lay the tiles in rows parallel to the wall, find the centre by marking across the room from the midpoints of opposite walls. Starting from the centre and working towards the walls, loose-lay a line of tiles. If a gap of less than a third of a tile width will be needed at each end of the row, remove the centre tile and adjust the rest of the tiles so that the now wider end tiles are the same width.

A diagonal arrangement, rather than one that runs parallel to the walls, can help disguise any defects such as uneven walls. To find the starting point with this arrangement, take two lengths of string and fix them diagonally across the room, from corner to corner. Place a corner of the first tile at the point where the two strings cross.

Use a spreader – usually supplied with the adhesive – to spread adhesive over about 1sq m (10sq ft), then lay the first tile. Carefully work your way towards the walls, ensuring that the tiles are kept in line and square to each other. When you get to the skirting board and have to cut a tile, place it directly over the last whole tile you laid. Take a third tile and place it against the skirting board and over the tile you want to cut. Mark a line on the second tile along the outer edge of the third tile (see diagram). Use a sharp trimming knife to cut the second tile along the marked line. To cut curves, first make a template out of paper or cardboard. When you've finished laying the tiles, walk all over the floor to make sure that the edges and corners are well stuck down.

To protect the tiles from wear, dirt and water once they have been laid, coat them with the liquid sealant recommended by the tile manufacturer.

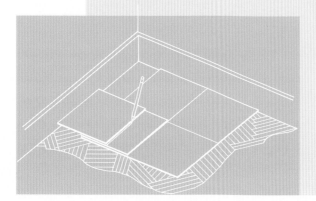

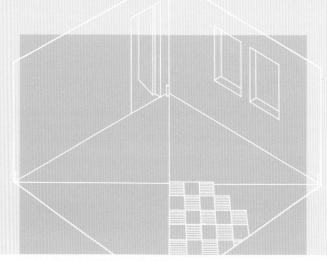

page 46   page 16

...make a **fake lime-stone** floor ☆☆☆

If you want your floor to look like limestone but not be cold underfoot, the easiest – and least expensive – solution is to make a replica out of 3mm (⅛in) MDF, cut into shapes and glued onto the existing floor. To do this, get a carpenter to lay a sheet of MDF on one half of the floor. Draw the shapes you want on the MDF, number them and have the carpenter cut them out. Loose-lay the shapes on the floor and mark round their edges with a felt-tip marker pen. Lay a second sheet of MDF on the other half of the

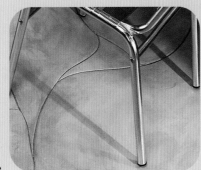

floor. Draw the shapes you want on this sheet so they link with the others like a giant jigsaw puzzle. Cut them out, loose-lay them and mark around their edges in the same way. Now take a Polaroid photo of the floor.

Referring to the photo and the numbers, fix each shape in place with flooring adhesive. When it has dried, prime with wood primer, and apply a coat of limestone-colour matt emulsion paint. Then colourwash the floor to create the limestone effect. Finally, give the floor several coats of acrylic eggshell varnish to protect the surface and give a limestone sheen.

...customize **your carpet** ☆☆☆

Customizing your carpet is a wonderful way of making inexpensive carpet look like a hand-woven masterpiece. Splicing two pieces together in a wavy design isn't difficult; you just need a bit of imagination and a good carpet fitter. But first things first. Before you even order any carpet, go to a carpet fitter with a rough drawing of the design you have in mind. If

your sketch elicits the 'I'm not so sure' response, then you'll need to look for another fitter.

Next, you must make a template – something that requires patience and a free afternoon. Take some lining paper and roll it out over the area where your design will be. If the paper isn't wide enough to accommodate your design, you'll need to stick several pieces together using masking tape. Mark out your design in pencil first. Drawing at this scale, it will probably take several attempts to get it right. The sky's the limit with the pattern – you could have fluid shapes, diamonds or other graphic shapes. When you are pleased with the pencil outline, draw over it with a dark marker pen. Cut out the template with scissors. Now it's time to show it to the carpet fitter and get his help with ordering the amount of carpet you'll need. When he comes to fit the carpet according to your design, make sure you are on hand to get it right.

...paint an African design ☆

Don't let your four walls hem you in. Open them up to the world with a painted-on design that takes its inspiration from the patterns and colours of Africa. First plan out the design you want and decide on its size and the colours you will use. This design has a caramel-coloured base, with terracotta, cobalt blue and brown. First apply the base colour using matt emulsion paint and leave it to dry thoroughly. Using a spirit level, straightedge and pencil, mark out a rectangle to the size of your choice. Mask off the rectangle with masking tape, then paint it in. When the paint is touch dry, carefully remove the masking tape. Then, once it has dried hard (you can speed this up rather niftily with a hair dryer), use a spirit level, straightedge and sharp pencil to mark on very fine vertical lines. Using these to guide you, paint on the wiggly freehand lines with an artist's brush. For best results, work quickly without hesitating. Finally, use your fingertips to apply the dots in a contrasting colour. When the paint is completely dry, remove the guidelines with a soft rubber.

...cover a wall with battens ☆☆

The attraction of this look is the contrast of the rough timber battens with the coloured wall behind. The wall must be painted before the battens are put in place. To estimate how many battens you'll need, first measure the width of the wall and divide that figure by the width of the battens you're using. As they are spaced a batten's-width apart, you then divide this last figure by two again. The final figure will be the number of battens required. For example, if the wall is 1320mm (4ft 4in) wide, divide this by the width of a batten (32mm) to get 41.25. Divide again by 2 to get 20.6, and round up to the nearest whole number, making 21 battens. Measure the length of the battens from the top of the skirting board to the ceiling, and buy lengths in the next largest size.

Leave the kiln-dried battens in the room for up to three weeks to acclimatize (see page 145). Cut the first batten to length. Start at a door or window and leave a gap equal to the width of a batten between the architrave and the first batten. Use an offcut of batten to measure the gap. Apply panel adhesive from a cartridge gun to the back of the first batten and fit it in place, using a spirit level to ensure that it is vertical. Nail in place too, then cut and fit the next batten in the same way. Repeat until the job is done.

page 37   page 95   page 108   page 121   page 106

...give a **rough effect** to your **walls** ☆☆☆

Dare to be different with walls plastered with a slightly rough surface to give them some gritty character. First get a plasterer in to cover your walls and ask him to leave the plaster with a slightly imperfect finish. Once the plaster is dry, paint the walls with a single coat of matt emulsion in your chosen colour. Apply this quite haphazardly with a large paintbrush so that the pink plaster still shows through here and there. Finally, give the walls two or three coats of acrylic eggshell varnish. This protects the paint and its slight sheen emphasizes the rough finish.

...transform a wall with **rendering** and **rope skirting** ☆☆☆

Feeling rough and ready? Here's an idea to bring a rustic, totally textural look to a room. The first step is to remove the skirting boards and any wallpaper, as concrete rendering will not bond to paper. Get a professional plasterer to apply the concrete rendering (you can also use plaster). To give him some idea of what you want, find an object such as a vase that has the rough-textured finish you require. Once the rendering is dry – this will take quite a while as it is a lot thicker than plaster – apply a coat of matt emulsion paint in a neutral colour, using a roller with a long-pile sleeve. You'll probably also need a brush to work paint into the deeper recesses. Finally, in place of the skirting board, fix thick rope to the floor with long oval nails. The heads of the nails will be hidden in the weave of the rope.

...make a **wall mosaic** ☆

A wall mosaic makes an interesting design feature and is cheaper than tiling an entire wall. Draw your design on the wall in pencil and use an artist's brush and matt emulsion paint to paint over the pencilled line. Allow the paint to dry. Use a glue gun to stick mosaic tiles randomly between the painted lines. If your mosaic tiles come in sheets with a paper backing, simply soak the sheets in water to dissolve the glue holding the paper. Make sure the tiles are completely dry before using them, otherwise they will not stick.

page 18   page 47   page 23

...paint **up and over colour** to a wall and ceiling ☆☆

A painted wall design that runs up and over the ceiling helps to give a room a unified feel, and can even continue over door and window frames. First use a spirit level and masking tape to mark out your blocks of colour. Start by sticking two vertical strips of tape on the wall to outline the colour block there. Then hold a set square against the ceiling in line with each of these two strips, and mark pencil guidelines on the ceiling to show where to position the masking tape for the block of ceiling colour. Decide where you want the design to finish and mask out at right-angles to the vertical strips.

Once you have marked out the blocks, paint them in using a large brush or a small paint roller with matt emulsion paint. Remove the masking tape when the paint is just touch-dry or else you risk removing the paint with it. Repeat for any further blocks of contrasting colour, making sure that each colour block is completely dry before starting on any overlapping blocks. Finally paint any door and window frames to match and finish these with several layers of matt acrylic varnish over the emulsion for protection.

...tile over **existing tiles** ☆☆

Tired of your tiles? Removing tiles from a whole room can be time-consuming and expensive, but provided your existing tiles are well fitted you can tile straight over the top. Thoroughly clean the old tiles with sugar soap to remove lime scale, soap residues and any mould that may be in the grout. Then simply tile over the old tiles as if you were working on bare plaster. The only thing you have to do differently is the grouting. Because the surface beneath is non-porous, the tile adhesive will take longer than usual to dry, so do not grout the gaps for a few days

To create a kaleidoscope effect, draw graphic shapes on the old tile surface with a marker pen. Then work upwards from the bottom, fitting the different coloured tiles at different angles as you go.

page 113   page 114   page 53

...paint a **glamorous gold wall** ☆

Give your bathroom walls the glamour treatment with this luxurious burnished effect. Paint the walls with red matt emulsion paint. Don't be tempted to paint over existing wallpaper because the dampness may make it lift. When the red paint is dry, it's time to apply the gold layer. Wet a small sponge with water and wring it out until most of the moisture is gone. Dab the sponge with the gold acrylic paint and then rub it onto the wall, using a circular motion. The trick is to apply a little at a time and build up the gold to the colour density that you want. It is a good idea to protect the finished surface from water splashes by applying two coats of clear acrylic varnish once the paint has dried.

...make a **wavy wall** ☆☆☆

Bring some fluidity to your walls with this clever construction. First you need a carpenter to build the profile that lies beneath the surface. This is made of four horizontal wave-shaped 'shelves', to which the 6mm (¼in) flexi-plywood (see diagram) is attached. The profile should have one straight edge. Make a template of it, deciding how many waves you want and get your carpenter to cut four times that number of 'shelves' from 9mm (⅜in) plywood. Screw them to horizontal wall battens positioned just below ceiling level, just above floor level and about one-third and two-thirds of the way up the wall. To anchor the flexi-plywood in the troughs at either side of every pair of waves, you need vertical wall battens made of 50 x 25mm (2 x 1in) softwood.

Once the profile is in place, apply woodworking adhesive to the curved edges of the 'shelves', and screw one vertical edge of a sheet of flexi-plywood to the first vertical wall batten. Now bend the flexi-plywood so it touches and sticks to the wave 'shelves', and press it into the next trough so you can screw it to its wall batten. Leave yourself room to screw the adpacent piece of plywood to the same batten. Countersink the screw holes and fill and sand them so that they will not be seen. Repeat the sequence to complete the wall, then paint with matt emulsion to finish.

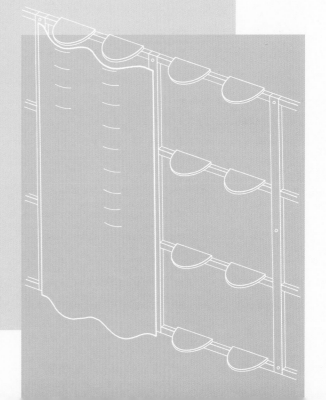

page 46   page 59, 60

...make a **curvy worktop** ☆☆

Why stand at a boring straight-edged worktop, when a curvy one like this will make you flow around the kitchen? First remove your existing kitchen worktop and replace it with a sheet of 9mm (⅜in) sandwich plywood. Make sure that the plywood extends at least 200mm (8in) beyond the front of

your kitchen units. Plan out your design, by drawing the curves you want in pencil on the plywood, ensuring that the curves do not come too close to your unit fronts. Cut the plywood using a jigsaw and sand the cut edges smooth with glasspaper or fine sandpaper.

Next, lay the plastic laminate on top of the plywood and pencil in the curves of the plywood on the underside of the laminate. Remove the laminate and carefully cut it using a jigsaw fitted with a fine blade, leaving 3mm (⅛in) between the cut and the pencilled line. Glue the laminate in position using laminate adhesive. Apply as much pressure as possible while the adhesive dries, to ensure a good bond between the two. Once it is dry, use glasspaper or fine sandpaper to smooth off the cut edges of the laminate.

You can adapt this technique to make laminate splashbacks, too. Follow the same procedure with plywood and laminate as above and fit the splashback in place using a fast-drying waterproof panel adhesive. Seal the gap between the worktop and the splashback with a length of slim quadrant moulding glued into place. Alternatively you can seal the gap with a bead of silicone mastic.

...paint a **household appliance** ☆

Who says a dishwasher or fridge has to be white? This will make your head reel and your eyes pop out, and it's easier to do than you think. First, thoroughly clean the appliance to remove any traces of dirt, grease and fingerprints. Mask off the parts that you don't want to paint, using masking tape and newspaper. Protect the floor with newspaper or a dust-sheet, then spray with metal primer. When dry, apply a coat

of solvent-based eggshell paint of your chosen colour, using a roller or an aerosol. Remove the masking tape when the paint is touch-dry and allow it to dry hard. Finally, paint on your own design using solvent-based paint. Be as wild as you possibly can or dare.

...decorate your **stairs** with **fallen leaves** ☆

This is an ideal and inexpensive alternative to replacing your stair carpet. Remove the carpet, tacks and staples, and fill and sand any holes. Prime the treads and risers, then, using a ruler as a guide, mask off the edges of the stairs. Give them two coats of matt emulsion paint, then remove the masking tape. When completely dry, mask off the inner area of the treads. Give this two coats of contrasting matt emulsion paint, then, before the paint has dried, carefully remove the masking tape so as not to damage the first colour.

This design uses leaf-shaped stencils and two colours, but you can choose any design and number of colours you like. As the stencils are quite small, you only need to use bits of masking tape to hold them in place. Dab on the first colour using a small sponge. Wait for this to dry before applying the second colour. Carefully lift off the stencil and repeat the process on each stair. When finished, apply at least five coats of acrylic varnish.

...fix **laminate** to doors ☆☆

Stuck with units you hate? Longing to inject some colour into your life? Don't despair. You can easily cover old unit doors with any laminate you please, to give them a new lease on life. And it's cheaper than replacing the cupboards, too. Start by measuring the door and mark out its dimensions on a sheet of laminate. Cut the laminate

to size using a jigsaw fitted with a fine blade, then sand the edges. Take the door off its hinges and lay it down flat. Check that the laminate is the right size, then apply an even coat of contact adhesive to the door and the laminate. When the adhesive is touch dry, lay the laminate in place. Press down firmly and evenly to get a good bond. To avoid any risk of the single sheet of laminate causing the cabinet door to warp, stick a balancing laminate on the door's inner face. You can use less expensive white laminate here. Replace the door when the adhesive is dry, and hey presto! A whole new look.

...fit aluminium **inserts** in doors ☆☆

Personalize your cupboard doors with these shiny metal inserts. Measure the door panels and, using a jigsaw fitted with a metal-cutting blade, cut the inserts from a 2mm (¹⁄₁₆in) thick sheet of perforated aluminium. Remove the doors from

the units and lay them flat on the floor. Apply small blobs of transparent silicone sealant to the underside of the inserts, then fit them in place. Allow the sealant to set and rehang the doors.

how to
windows

...make a **modern stained-glass** window ☆

Being overlooked by neighbours is a common problem throughout the home, but the glass traditionally used for privacy in bathrooms is often uninspiring, to say the least. A modern stained-glass effect like this is simple and inexpensive. It works best on flat-surface window glass.

Get several sheets of long-lasting translucent and opaque self-adhesive vinyl in a variety of different colours. Vinyl is usually used for outdoor shop displays and so is completely waterproof – ideal for the bathroom. Clean and dry the window, then cut out the rectangular vinyl shapes. You can make other shapes if you want. Peel off the backing paper and press them onto the glass in a haphazard fashion. Overlap some to create new colourways and to make sure that the glass is completely covered.

...make **fretwork** shutters ☆☆☆

These shutters were designed to disguise the plain yet effective double-glazed windows of a bathroom and to echo the oval shape of the mirrors, but you can adapt the design to suit your room. Measure your window recess and give these measurements and a sketch of the pattern you want to a company specializing in making fretwork (you will find local firms listed in Yellow Pages under Fretwork – or see stockists). Ask the company to send you a drawing – or better still, a computer-generated image – of the finished design for your approval. Ask to have the shutters ready-primed for painting. When they are delivered, use masking tape and newspaper to mask off the framework, leaving just the ovals. Making sure the room you work in is well ventilated, spray-paint the ovals using a water-based aerosol paint. You will have to spray several times from different angles to ensure they are well covered. Remove the masking when the paint is touch-dry. Paint the framework and finally, have a carpenter fix the shutters in position and fit a handle to each.

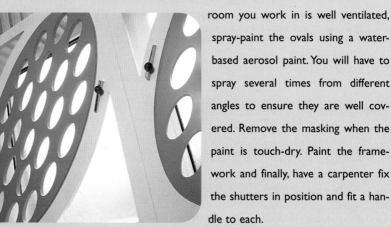

page 93, 95   page 123   page 98   page 54   page 108

...fit **sandblasted glass** to a window ☆☆☆

If you need total privacy but also want as much natural light as possible, sheets of sandblasted glass fitted over the existing windows are your answer. Measure the windows of your room to the outside of the recess, add 10cm (4in) to each measurement, and give the measurements to a glass merchant. Ask him to supply you with a sheet of toughened, sandblasted glass for each window, each with six holes for fixing. Fix the glass to the wall using large roundhead screws and rubber washers. If you want to be able to open your windows, get hinges fixed to the sheets of sandblasted glass instead of having holes drilled, and mount the glass on the wall using the hinges.

...**etch** on **glass** ☆

Having glass acid-etched by a glass merchant is expensive, but there is an aerosol spray which gives the effect of acid-

etching at a fraction of the cost. Using 6mm (¼in) wide masking tape, mask out your design on the back of the glass. Rub your finger along the tape to make sure it is firmly in place, otherwise the finished lines may not have enough definition. Mask off any surround (the window or door frame) using masking tape and newspaper. Spray a coat of the paint etching agent back and forth and up and down the glass. You must apply several light coats, rather than one heavy one. Re-spray every five minutes until you have achieved the desired effect. Allow it to dry completely and then carefully remove the masking tape from the frame and from the glass. Use a clean, dry paintbrush to get rid of any flakes of dry agent which fall as the plastic masking tape is removed. The etched side of the glass must be cleaned gently from now on, as it's nowhere near as robust as the real thing, but it looks great and costs very little!

...design a **stained-glass** window ☆☆☆

Windows are generally overlooked when it comes to room decoration. Sure you'll slap a fresh coat of paint on the window frame and maybe hang new curtains or a blind, but what about the glass itself? We tend to take it for granted because we don't really see it. But why not give it some character of its own in the shape of a piece of stained glass? Your inspiration for a design can come from any source: magazines, books about plants or wildlife, museums and galleries are just a few of the possibilities. When you've decided on the design you'd like, draw a rough sketch and choose the colours. Contact a designer of stained glass who will come and measure up your window and make your dream come true!

...make an **abstract** light ☆☆☆

An abstract light of your own design allows you to make your mark on a room without having to splash your cash on expensive light fittings. Draw out your design on a 6mm (¼in) sheet of MDF and cut out the shape with a jigsaw. You could have a single board with shapes cut out of it (see right) or a thin curly shape to defuse the light more subtly. Use small nails and glue to fix a 100mm (4in) strip of 3mm (⅛in) plywood to the edge of the shape to give the illusion of thickness. Take

several small blocks of wood – as many as you will need to suspend the board from the ceiling – and screw a cuphook to each block. Glue and screw these to the upper surface of the board. These will have chain attached to suspend the shape from the ceiling. To locate the positions on the ceiling for the cuphooks from which the light will hang, refer to How to Make an Arc Light (opposite). Fix cuphooks to the ceiling at the marked points using wallplugs. Suspend the shape from the ceiling with equal lengths of chain. To finish, ask an electrician to fit a light fitting to the top surface of the abstract shape.

...make a **billowing** light cover ☆

Make waves and hide an ugly ceiling light fitting with this easy-to-make billowing light cover. Not only is it better looking than a bare light bulb, but it will also diffuse the light to give a gentle glow to your room. First decide on the width and length of fabric that you want to use. You can use balloon fabric or any flame-retardant fabric. Sew casings wide enough to hold a piece of 10mm (⅜in) wooden dowel into either end of the fabric. Cut four equal lengths of dowel, 400mm (16in) longer than the width of the fabric. Using wallplugs, fix four pairs of cuphooks to the ceiling, two pairs either side of the light. The distance between each one of a pair must be 200mm (8in) less than the length of the dowels. Slide a length of dowel into the casings at each end of the fabric and suspend these from the outer pairs of cuphooks. Fit the two

centre lengths of dowel on their cuphooks and adjust the fabric so it is evenly draped over them.

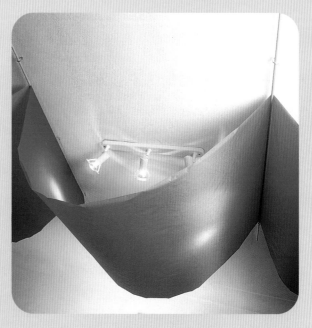

...make an **arc light** ☆☆☆

Spread light around by using this fitting that runs three lamps from the same cable. Cut an arc shape out of 12mm (½in) MDF. Drill three holes large enough to take the cable, then pin and glue a 100mm (4in) wide strip of 3mm (⅛in) MDF around the edge to give the arc some depth.

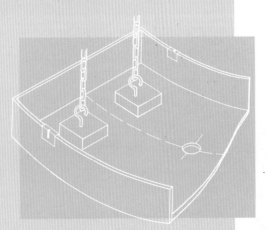

Paint with two coats of matt emulsion. On the top surface, mark the midpoint of each of the short sides and join these with a line that is the arc's centre line (see diagram).

Screw a cuphook into each of six small blocks of wood, then glue and screw them to the arc's top surface, equally spaced along the centre line. Stick masking tape to the sides of the arc next to each block and mark a line on each piece (see diagram). Measure the distance between each cuphook and its masking tape. Now hold the arc up, centred below the existing ceiling socket, and mark the ceiling where the six pencil lines touch it. Measure in from these points the same distance as from the tape to the cuphooks, and mark these new points. They are the ceiling fixing points. Use hooks with spring-toggle fixing devices to carry the weight of the arc and lights. Cut six lengths of chain. Attach them to the cuphooks on the arc, then suspend the fitting from the hooks on the ceiling. Get an electrician to attach three lamps to the arc, wire them up to a junction box on top and connect this to the existing flex to power the lights.

...reposition a **ceiling light** ☆☆☆

A central light as the main source in a room is seldom anything other than functional. Moving it to somewhere more attractive can be costly and messy, but instead you could simply extend the flex from the ceiling rose, hook it up elsewhere, and make the loop of flex into a decorative feature in its own right. Unless you feel absolutely confident dealing with electrics, extending the flex is a job that should be left to an electrician. Once you have a longer flex to play around with, screw a cuphook into the ceiling at the spot where you want the light to hang and loop the cable through it. The hook must go into a ceiling joist or a cavity-fixing device such as a spring toggle; if you screw it into plasterboard it will soon pull out. Fix another cuphook near the spot where the flex emerges from the ceiling, then hang decorative chain from one hook to the other, wrapping it around the flex to make it look like an integral part of the design – which it is!

how to
mirrors & things

...make a **Hollywood-style** mirror ☆

Mirror, mirror, on the wall…but why stop at just one mirror? Why not multiply the glamour rating with lots of extra little

ones? First buy a round mirror of the size you want, bearing in mind that, when the design is complete, it will be larger. Hold the mirror in place on the wall and use a pencil to draw round the bottom half. Hammer several large nails into the wall along the marked line. Don't

hammer them all the way in, but instead leave about 30mm (1¼in) exposed. Apply a large squiggle of mirror adhesive — available from glass merchants — to the back of the mirror. Sit the mirror on the nails and press firmly in place against the wall. The nails will stop the mirror from falling, but prop something such as a broom handle against the mirror to hold it in place for about 24 hours while the adhesive sets. Once it is dry, remove the nails, fill the holes and touch up. The mosaic mirrors come in sheets attached to a hessian backing. Cut through the hessian to give you individual pieces, then stick them around the mirror using sticky mirror fixers. A random design looks best.

...make an **abstract mirror** ☆☆☆

Make a template of the shape of frame you require, and another smaller one for the inner opening, where the mirror will fit. Trace the design onto a piece of 25mm (1in) birch sandwich plywood and cut it out, using a jigsaw. Stain the frame with several coats of water-based woodstain. Take the

inner template to your mirror supplier and have them cut the mirror for you, 50mm (2in) larger all round than the template. Lay the frame face down and stick the mirror to the back of it using special mirror adhesive, which will not damage the silver backing of the mirror. Use an offcut of plywood and several tins of paint to weight the mirror down while the adhesive is drying.

...decorate a **mirror with studs** ☆

The studs used here look like individual studs, but actually come in strips approximately 1m (3ft) long. Every fifth one has a hole in it through which a real stud is hammered to hold the strip in place. The advantage is less hammering, and it is easier to keep the lines of studs straight. To decorate a mirror, fix a first row of studs along the edge of the frame

closest to the mirror. To position the second row of studs, use a ruler and pencil to mark a series of points 25mm (1in) from the centre of the first row. Use these points as a guide when nailing the second row in place. Fix a third row 25mm (1in) from the second in the same way.

page 114   page 107   page 23   page 17   page 24

...make your own works of art ☆

Express your artistic talent and let your friends believe you've spent a fortune on modern art. Choose from runny, painted canvases (see right) – three in a row look especially chic – or a three-dimensional string sculpture (see left). Or you can paint your own design. All of them start with blank artist's canvases bought from an artist's supplier. For the runny pictures, simply lean the canvas against a wall, protect the wall and floor with plastic sheeting, then run a paintbrush loaded with matt emulsion along the top edge. Leave the paint to do its own thing. For the string picture you need to start by painting the canvas in the colour of your choice. When it's dry, simply attach string of different thicknesses using a glue gun. As the string is sold in balls, it will naturally form itself into coils when you unwind it.

...make a jazzy fretwork panel ☆☆☆

To bring new life to an old staircase, why not replace the side balustrade with a jazzy fretwork panel? The first step is to measure the distance between the underneath of the handrail and the top of the base rail at several points along the staircase. Then measure the distance between each newel post. Give this information, together with a sketch of the design you want, to a company specializing in fretwork (look in Yellow Pages under Fretwork, or see stockists). There are Building Regulations governing staircase balustrades, so the panel must be made from strong board and any gaps in the design should be no more than 100mm (4in). The fretwork company may be able to send you a computer-generated drawing of the finished panel for your approval before they go ahead. Ask them to prime and paint the finished panel.

Meanwhile, remove your spindles by sawing them level with the handrail at the top, and with the base rail at the bottom. Sand and fill any holes. When your panel is delivered, fix it in place by screwing it firmly into the underside of the handrail and down into the base rail at regular intervals, and to the faces of the newel posts.

page 17   page 81

...frame a **picture collection** with **bamboo** ☆☆

Eighteen pictures all together on a wall pack quite a punch, but to give them a sense of unity, try arranging them around a central wall light and adding bamboo framing. First use a spirit level and a straightedge and pencil to mark out your rectangle. Mine was 3060mm (120in) across and 1380mm

(55in) high, which is 120mm (4in) higher and 1140mm (42in) wider than the area the pictures will cover. Find the centre of the rectangle and get an electrician to fix the light at this point. (You can, of course, work around an existing light fitting.)

To make the crossed bamboo decoration beneath the light, lash together with string two pieces of bamboo. Stand them on the floor, drill through the inside top of each and fix to the wall with screws and wallplugs.

My picture frames are 320mm (13in) wide and 420mm (17in) deep. To position them, I started with the column nearest the light. I wanted the edge of the first picture 30mm (1in) from the top of the crossed bamboo decoration, so I marked a point 190mm (7½in) – that's 30mm (1in) plus 160mm (6½in), half the width of the frame – from the edge of the bamboo. This point gave a vertical guideline for the picture hooks hanging the first column of pictures.

The mid-line of the second column of pictures is 450mm (18in) from the mid-line of the first column – 160mm (6½in) for half the width of the frame, plus 130mm (5in) for the width of the bamboo, plus another 160mm (6½in) to the mid-line of the second column. Mark this point,

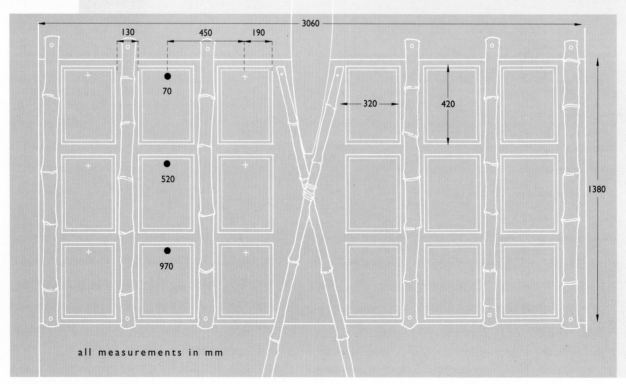

3060

130   450   190

70

520

970

320   420

1380

all measurements in mm

then measure the same distance on for the third column. Repeat the whole process on the other side of the light.

You now have six points. Using a pencil, spirit level and straightedge, draw vertical guidelines from each of these points down to the bottom of the marked-out rectangle. Next mark the positions of the picture hooks. On my frames, the fixing was 40mm (2in) from the top of each frame. Starting at the top of each vertical line, I marked points 70mm (3in), 520mm (21in) and 970mm (39in) down from the top. The height of my rectangle was 1380mm (55in), so three

frames 420mm (17in) deep gives a height of 1260mm (51in), plus a 30mm (1in) gap above and below each frame matched the rectangle height exactly. Repeat on each of the other five marked lines, and fix the picture hooks in place.

Now it's time to mask off the rectangle and paint it in. Extend the paint beyond the edge of the last picture frame by about 250mm (10in) each side. The paint will cover all the pencil marks. When dry, hang the 18 pictures. Finally, fix the upright bamboos by drilling inside them through their tops and bottoms and screwing them to the wall, using wallplugs.

...make a message board ☆

Short of wall space – then why not make use of your win-

dow area? This is made very simply from a lightweight picture frame (with an acrylic rather than glass front) and self-adhesive lettering. Remove the cardboard picture backing from the frame. Use the lettering to print the days of the week on the front of the acrylic sheet. Then fix just the sheet in the frame, using the small metal fittings that usually hold the backing in place.

Fit two cuphooks to the back of the frame, close to each top corner. Hang the frame from a slat of a Venetian blind. If the slat bends slightly, fix a piece of cardboard or small block of wood with double-sided sticky tape between the slat and the one below behind each hook. This will spread the weight of the frame onto the two slats so the top slat will no longer bend. The blocks can be removed when you close the blinds.

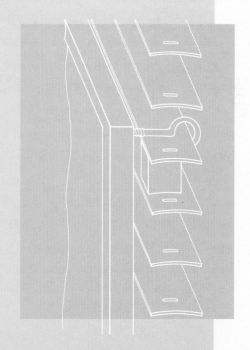

If you have vertical slats, they should be able to carry the weight without bending. If you don't have blinds, you can suspend the notice board from the ceiling with fishing line, which will be invisible. Once it is finished, use your message boards to attach self-adhesive notes.

...make a **pod table** ☆☆☆

The secret of this table is bendy MDF. The design consists of three main sections: the table top, the ceiling panel (which have the same dimensions) and the wall panel (the size of which will depend on the height of your ceiling).

Cut two rectangles the same size from a sheet of 25mm (1in) MDF for the table top and ceiling panel. Use a jigsaw to round off the two front corners of each panel to a quarter circle. Attach two legs to the underside of the table top with adhesive and drive four screws down through the table top into the top of each leg for extra strength. Screw a 50 x 25mm (2 x 1in) batten horizontally to the wall 25mm (1in) higher than the tops of the legs, then screw the table top to it from underneath. The batten will eventually be covered by the curved inner surface and filled to be hidden from view.

Measure the distance from the level of the table top up to the ceiling. Cut a piece of 25mm (1in) board this long and as wide as the table top for the wall panel, and fix it to the wall above the table top using screws and wallplugs. Get an electrician to run cable to the ceiling above the table, then fix the ceiling panel to the ceiling, selecting the screw positions so they go into the joists.

Cut a sheet of 6mm (¼in) bendy MDF to cover the table top, the wall panel and the ceiling panel. Pin and glue it in place with panel pins and woodworking adhesive to give the smooth, curved line of the inside of the pod. Cut lilac plastic laminate sheeting to the same size, and glue it in place over the bendy MDF using contact adhesive. Round off the front

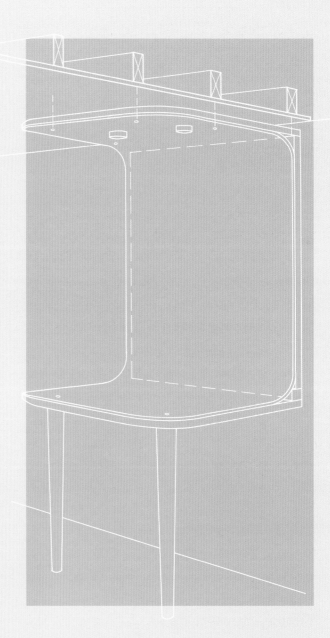

corners of the bendy MDF and laminate, then sand the edges ready for painting. To fill behind the curve and the wall panel, cut two pieces of MDF to the same shape, then pin and glue to each side. Paint to finish.

The final step is to get an electrician to wire up and install the light fittings in the top of the pod.

page 59   page 46

...make a **suspended table** ☆☆

Who needs table legs when you can float your table top in mid-air (well, almost!). This table must be suspended from the ceiling joists as quite a lot of tension is needed on the rigging cables to keep them taut. Start by cutting out your desired shape from 25mm (1in) thick sandwich plywood, and prime and paint it. Locate the joists above the planned position of your table by tapping the ceiling – a dull sound indicates a joist. Confirm the joist positions precisely by making test drillings with a small twist drill. Place the table top on the floor and suspend four lengths of thread, each weighted with a small nut or similar obpect, from the ceiling with drawing pins. Move them along the lines of the joists until the weights are evenly spaced over the table top.

Mark the positions of the weights on the table top. At each mark, drill a hole 1mm (1/16) larger in diameter than the wire through the table top, and into the floor so that the holes can act as fixing guides for the bottom eye plates. Move the table top out of the way. Remove the threads; leave the drawing pins to mark the locations of the top eye plates on the ceiling. Screw the plates to the ceiling and the floor at the marked positions. Measure the distance from floor to ceiling, add 200mm (8in), and cut four lengths of 3mm (1/8in) diameter cable to this measurement with wire cutters. Loop a length of cable through each of the ceiling eye plates and use cable grips to secure the cable to itself.

Fit a cable tensioning device called a turnbuckle or bottle screw to each of the four floor eye plates. Rest the table top on a box at roughly the level you want it and thread the four cables down through the holes you drilled earlier. Slide a plain washer and a screw-on bush onto each cable from the bottom, thread the cable through the turnbuckle, pull it tight and secure it to itself using another cable grip. Slide each washer and bush up its cable and tighten the screws on the bush to lock it onto the cable against the underside of the table top. Remove the box and make the cables taut by tightening the turnbuckles. Adjust the height of your table by loosening the bushes and sliding them up or down the cables as necessary. Use a spirit level to ensure that the table top is level before tightening the bushes fully.

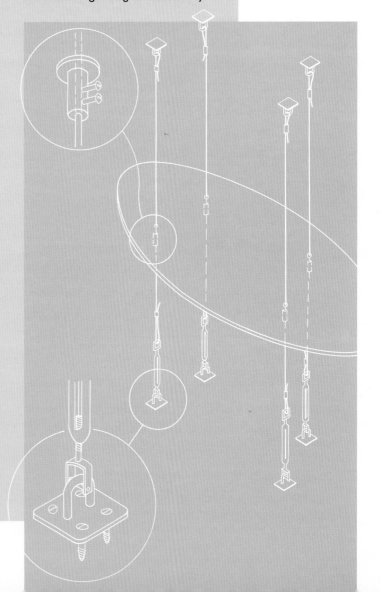

page 26   page 23

...make a coffee table **on castors** ☆☆

Ever seen a table that thinks it's a skateboard? Well here it is. When you've finished having your coffee on it, you can use it to skate away! First cut a sheet of 19mm (¾in) shuttering board in half widthways and hold the two pieces together with masking tape to create a double thickness. Mark out your chosen shape on it in pencil and cut it out with a jigsaw. Sand any rough edges. Now position four large castors upside down on the top surface near the corners of your shape. Mark where the holes should go, drill pilot holes right

through the board and then attach the castors to the underside. Now remove the masking tape – the screws holding the castors will also hold the sandwich of board together. Apply a coat of watered-down matt emulsion and, so you still see grain, before it has dried wipe over the surface in one direction with a clean, soft cloth. When the paint is dry, give it two coats of varnish.

...make a **console table/ radiator cover** ☆☆

One of the problems with radiator covers is that they cut down on the heat given out. This one doesn't and has the added benefit of being a very stylish narrow console table. The front is made from fallen branches collected on a walk through a wood. To make the table, cut two matching pieces of 19mm (¾in) sandwich plywood for the top using a jigsaw. Each piece should have a long straight edge that will butt up to the wall. Fix a 50mm (2in) square batten, 100mm (4in) shorter than the long edge of the plywood, to the wall above the radiator and screw one of the pieces of plywood to its top. Cut the branches to length so they fit between the underside of the plywood and the floor. Fix them to the underside of the plywood using screws driven down through the surface and into the top of

each individual branch. You may have to drill a hole in each branch first to avoid splitting the wood.

When all the branches are in position, glue the second piece of plywood on top of the first with woodworking adhesive. This means that none of the screw holes will be visible from the top. Stain the top using several coats of water-based woodstain.

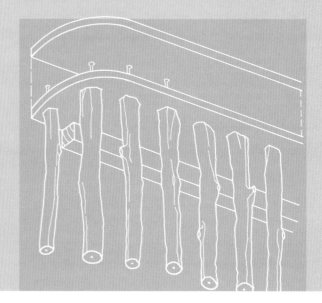

page 74

...build a **desk** in a **tight spot** ☆☆

Here's a desk that reaches those places other desks don't reach. There are two main stages to this project; building the desktop, and adding the shelves. The desktop is made from piece of 19mm (¾in) MDF, with one end rounded off. Cut the board to fit your space, then screw 50mm (2in) square wall battens to the door and window wall at the level you want the desktop to be. Screw it onto the batten, then position the supporting leg by driving screws down through the surface into the top of the leg to hold it securely. Countersink all the screw holes so that they can be filled, sanded and painted in order to make a smooth work surface.

To make the sliding keyboard, cut a shelf from 12mm (½in) MDF to match your keyboard width, and fit it on side-mounted drawer runners between two 50 x 25mm (2 x 1in) wood supports. Slide this whole assembly underneath the desktop from the front, then drive screws down through the upper surface into the wooden supports. Complete the desktop by pinning and gluing two strips of 3mm (⅛in) plywood to the front edge of the desktop surface as a fascia to hide the construction. If you wish, you can buy ready-made keyboard shelves from superstores (see stockists).

The tall shelf unit is made up from two uprights and four shelves pinned and glued together. Stand it at the end of the worktop, and secure it to the wall with two mirror plates attached to the rear edge of the uprights. In this room, the light switch had to be moved from the wall next to the door frame in order to free up the wall space for the shelf unit –

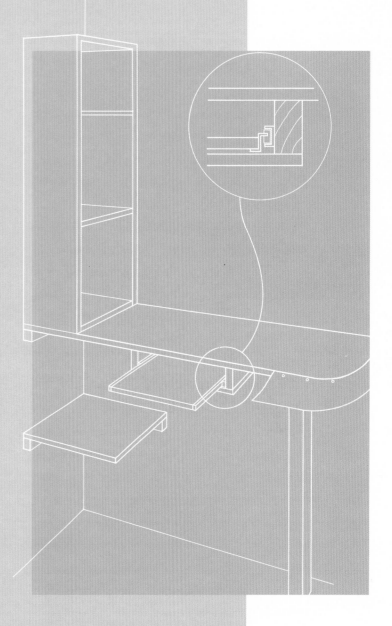

a job for an electrician unless you are competent at doing wiring work.

The extra shelf below the worktop simply rests on two wall battens. Finally, attach the support bracket for the computer monitor to the free end of the desktop, and make sure that all cables are hidden from view by taping them to the underside of the desk.

how to
fireplaces

...install a **glass bowl** fire ☆☆☆

Add some life to a boring old fire-place opening by making this snazzy electric-powered alternative to a real fire. With nothing much more than a large, shallow glass bowl, some light bulbs and a few cobbles, you will have a bright focal point to your room that doesn't need its coals raked or its ash removed. Find a glass bowl that will fit into your fireplace opening. Get an electrician to run a length of flex into the back of the fireplace, making sure that it is out of sight, and to connect it to an on-off switch and a further length of flex.

Take the bowl to a glazier and have a hole drilled through the base for the flex to pass through. Then stand the bowl on its bed of cobbles and run the flex into it. Get your electrician to connect the flex via a junction box to lam-pholders for three light bulbs. Fill the bowl with more loose bulbs for decoration. When the electricity is turned on, these will diffuse the light from the three working bulbs to give the fireplace a warm glow.

...make a simple **fireplace** and **hearth** ☆☆☆

If you want to replace an old fireplace with a modern one, it's not as difficult as you may think. (You must check though whether the building is Grade I listed before taking out an existing fireplace.) Have the original surround removed and the wall made good, and get a gas fitter to install a gas pipe into the opening. Decide on the size of surround you want, and fix a framework of 38mm (1½in) square support battens to the wall to which you can fix vertical and horizontal strips of 12mm (½in) MDF. Then fit the one-piece face panel of the fire surround to the edges of these strips using woodwork-ing adhesive and 25mm (1in) panel pins. Line the inner faces of the surround with fireproof 25mm (1in) cement board, then paint the entire structure with matt emulsion.

Build up the hearth with a sand-and-cement mix to a minimum depth of 500mm (20in) beyond the fire surround, leaving it with a rough finish for a more natural and tactile

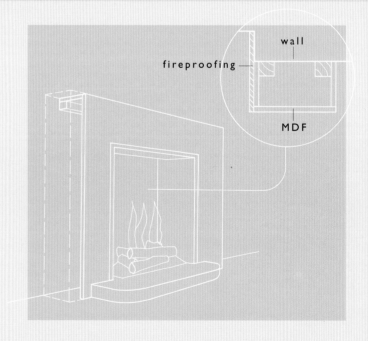

look. Make up a simple mould from timber to contain the sand and cement while it sets. Complete the job by having a fuel-effect gas fire installed by your fitter. You will have to repaint the back of the opening regularly if you use the fire.

page 18   page 39   page 78

...install a glass mantelshelf ☆☆☆

A mantelshelf does not have to be in the conventional position above the fireplace. Try flouting convention and positioning one beneath instead. This hole-in-the-wall gas flame-effect fire has an under-hung mantelshelf made of 25mm (1in) float glass with a rounded polished edge. The shelf needs to be about 200mm (8in) longer than the width of the fire opening.

First make a template out of stiff cardboard to your own design. Add 50mm (2in) to the depth of the template along its straight edge – this portion of the mantelshelf will be set into a slot cut in the wall. Have your shelf cut to shape by a glass merchant. Using a spirit level and straightedge, mark a horizontal line beneath the fireplace where you want to

position the mantelshelf. Mark the position of the slot on the wall, and chop it out with a hammer and a cold chisel. It needs to be as long as the mantelshelf and about 40mm (1½in) high and 50mm (2in) deep. You can make it easier to chop out the masonry if you first drill a series of closely spaced holes within the slot outline.

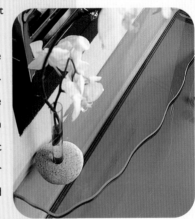

Slide the glass into the slot and pack with a sand-and-cement mix, making sure the mantelshelf is propped in place and kept level while it sets. When dry, plaster over the sand-and-cement mix and paint the wall.

...decorate a fireplace with smashed tiles ☆

Get smashing for a cheap and cheerful way of bringing life to a fire surround without the hassle of ripping out the entire structure. Choose tiles that match your decorating scheme to give you an interior-decorator look, or go for a complete contrast if you prefer to startle your friends. You can even do this project straight on top of existing tiling if you wish. However, you will need to clean them thoroughly with sugar soap first to remove residues, as well as leaving more time for the adhesive to dry before grouting.

Measure the area that you want to tile and buy an equal number of black and white ceramic tiles (as I used here) to cover it. Put them in a strong plastic shopping bag and use a hammer to break them up. The bag will protect you from any flying bits of tile.

Spread an even layer of tile adhesive on the surround. Work on an area about the size of a sheet of A4 paper at a time to make sure the adhesive doesn't set faster than you can work. Position the pieces of tile one by one, taking care not to cut yourself on the sharp edges. Leave gaps between the pieces for the grout.

Let the adhesive dry overnight, then use a sponge to apply grout. Using a fresh sponge, wipe off any excess grout, then leave to dry. Wipe down with a damp cloth to remove any remaining grout, then polish with a dry cloth.

how to
screens

...make a **fabric screen** ☆☆

Now here's an easy alternative to having the builders in to build a wall for you: a sliding screen of fabric panels that doesn't require planning permission and can easily be taken down when you move. You can make as many panels as you like, but this screen has three.

Measure the width of the room at the point where you want the screen to hang. Divide this measurement by three to give you the width of each of the panels. Next measure for the height of the screen. Don't forget to allow for a small gap between the top of the panels and the ceiling, and the bottom and the floor. Using these measurements, make three fabric panels with casings top and bottom to take a length of 10mm (½in) wooden dowel. The dowel at the top will keep the panels straight, and the one at the bottom will weight the fabric down. Cut six pieces of dowel to the width of the fabric and slide them into the casings. Then screw a cuphook

through the fabric into the dowel at each end at the top of each screen. These will be used to hang the panels on the cable, which is a length of 2mm (¹⁄₁₆in) diameter cable running across the room, back and then across again (see diagram). Buy enough cable to span the room three times. You will also

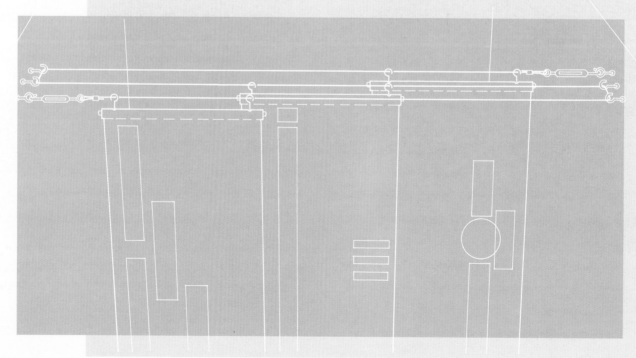

page 28   page 32

need two tensioning devices called turnbuckles or bottle screws, two cable grips, two screw eyes and four cuphooks (see picture).

Drill three holes approximately 50mm (2in) deep and about 15mm (½in) apart at the required height on the two walls between which the screens will hang. Insert a heavy-duty wallplug into each hole, then fit one screw eye and two cuphooks on each wall (see picture). Use a cable grip to attach one end of the cable to the closed eye of the first turnbuckle. Hook it onto a screw eye and thread the cable back and forth across the room through the four cuphooks. Fit the other turnbuckle to the other end of the cable and attach this to the screw eye on the opposite wall. Hang one fabric panel from each stretch of cable. Tension the cable by rotating the bodies of the turnbuckles with a screwdriver inserted in their slots until the panels hang level. Then you can slide the panels of the screen back and forth across the room as you please.

...screen off a TV ☆☆

A TV is an ugly beast at the best of times, so why not camouflage it with a decorative screen, made of hinged panels of painted MDF? The first thing to do is work out how many panels your screen will need to hide the TV. Put the TV on the floor, then cut several lengths of masking tape, each approximately 300mm (12in) long. Stick the strips of tape end to end on the floor in a concertina shape around the front three sides of the TV (see diagram). Each strip represents the position of a panel. Once you are happy with your layout, you will be able to see how many panels you need. The height of the panels can be easily judged by adding about 100mm (4in) to the height of the TV and its stand or table. Once you have planned out your design, you are ready to make it up. Alternatively, you can have the panels made by a company specializing in fretwork (see under Fretwork in Yellow Pages, or see stockists).

Mark out the panels on a sheet of MDF. Cut them to the correct width with a handsaw or a jigsaw and sand the edges smooth. Then mark off the height, draw the shape of the top on each one, and cut along the lines with your jigsaw. Finally, make a cardboard template for the cut-outs, transfer the design to each panel and use your jigsaw to cut them out. Join the panels together with butt hinges concertina-fashion, then spray-prime and spray-paint the screen to finish.

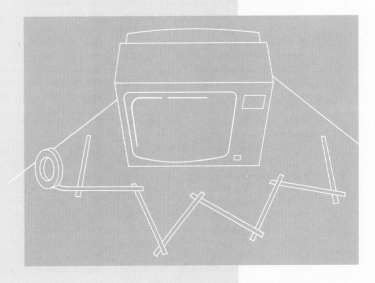

builders' jargon

It's all too easy to be baffled by builders' jargon. Here are some terms you may come across:

Acrow prop   Adjustable support used to hold up parts of a building while work is carried out underneath.

Architrave   Wood moulding fitted between a door or window frame and the surrounding wall.

Batten   Rectangular piece of softwood.

Beading   Narrow strip of wood used for edging or decoration.

Beam   Load-bearing piece of timber, reinforced concrete or steel.

Bevel   Angle or slope on a surface.

Bit   Drill bit for making holes.

Carriage   Strong piece of timber used to support the treads and risers beneath a wide staircase.

Casement   Hinged opening frame containing glass, forming part of a casement window.

Cavity wall   House wall consisting of two brick or block walls with a cavity between them, often now filled with insulating material.

Chalk line   String coated in coloured chalk, used for marking guidelines on wall and ceiling surfaces especially when paperhanging, and on floors when tiling.

Concrete   Mixture of sand, cement and gravel (aggregate).

Coping   Overhanging top of a wall, fitted to protect the wall from rain.

Countersinking   Widening the top of a screw hole in a cone shape so the screw head fits flush to the surface.

Dado rail   Moulding usually fitted horizontally at waist height along a wall.

Damp proof course   Waterproof layer built into a house wall close to ground level to stop damp rising; often abbreviated to DPC.

Directional light   Adjustable light fitting designed to illuminate objects or work surfaces.

Door stop   Battens fitted to the sides and top of a door frame against which the door closes.

Dowel   Machined timber rod used to join two pieces of wood together.

Downlighter   Ceiling light that shines a beam of light downwards.

Filler   Paste used for filling holes.

Fillet   Triangular piece of wood used between mouldings.

Flashing   Metal sheet or strip used to cover the join between the roof and another surface such as a chimney stack.

Flaunching   Shaped mortar top of a chimney to keep the rain out.

Flex   Insulated electrical wire used for connecting lamps and appliances to the mains.

Galvanized   Metal which has been given a protective coating of zinc.

Glazing   Technique of fitting glass in windows.

Grommet   A rubber ring or metal casing fitted around the inside of a hole to protect cables passing through the hole from chafing.

In-situ   Furniture made in position.

Joining plate   Rectangular piece of metal used to join or repair wood.

Joist   Beam of timber, steel or concrete used to carry a floor or ceiling.

Joist hanger   Metal shoe used to support the end of a joist.

Knotting   Sealer applied over the knots in wood before painting.

Lath   Thin strip of wood used to make a framework support for plaster and tiles.

Lintel   Beam above a window or door to support the wall above.

Louvred window   Window containing parallel strips of glass that overlap when closed.

Mastic   A pliable moisture-resistant substance used to seal joins.

MDF (medium density fibreboard)   Man-made board consisting of wood fibres bonded together under pressure with adhesive.

Mitre   Corner joint of two pieces of wood, formed by cutting bevels of equal angles at the ends of each piece.

Mortar   Mixture of sand and cement, used for laying bricks and rendering walls.

Newel post   Post which supports the handrail at the top and bottom of stairs.

Noggin   Solid block of wood placed between floor joists or timber wall studs for added support.

Nosing   Rounded edge of a step.

Parapet   Low wall or railing at the edge of a roof.

Parting bead   Shaped piece of wood fitted at the sides of a sliding sash window to keep the two sashes apart.

Pelmet   Decorative structure used to cover the top of a curtain.

Plasterboard   Sheet material used to form the surface of walls and ceilings.

Pointing   Narrow mortar visible between bricks or blocks in a wall.

Pre-cast   Made in a particular form before use; usually refers to concrete work.

Pre-stressed concrete   Concrete that has extra strength due to tensioned metal rods or wires embedded in its core.

Purlin   Horizontal beam supporting roof rafters.

Rafter   Sloping beam forming part of a roof.

Rail   Horizontal framing member in a window or door.

Rebate   Groove cut in a piece of timber.

Riser   Vertical part of a step.

Rot   Decay in timber. Dry rot is a fungus that takes the moisture out of timber, causing it to weaken. Wet rot is caused by too much moisture.

Sash   Frame of door or window containing glass.

Scrim   Linen mesh used in plastering to mask joints.

Sill   The shaped bottom part of a window or door frame.

Soffit   Underside of a stair, an arch or overhanging eaves.

Span   The distance between two supports.

Stay   Window catch that holds a casement window open.

Stud   Vertical timber in a stud partition wall.

Template   Shaped pattern used to cut around an object.

Tongue and groove   Interlocking planks in which one edge of each plank is shaped to form a tongue and the other edge is grooved.

Tread   Flat section of a step.

Uplighter   Lamp or wall light designed to cast light upwards.

Veneer   Thin wood or other decorative material used to cover rough or plain wood.

Wallplate   Timber built into a wall to provide support for joists or rafters.

Kitchen Glossary

When standing in a kitchen showroom, you can easily become mesmerized by technical speak. Below are some common kitchen terms:

Adjustable legs   Short supports beneath kitchen base units which can be extended or retracted to get the units level on uneven floors.

Built-in   Domestic appliances with no top or side panels, which can be fitted flush within their housing units.

Carcass   Basic framework of a kitchen wall or base unit, usually made from melamine-faced chipboard.

Carousel   Shelf system for corner cupboards, consisting of two circular shelves which rotate on a central pole and provide accessible storage.

Convection oven   Oven with a fan that circulates hot air evenly and speeds up the cooking process.

Corian   Durable man-made resin used to make moulded one-piece sinks and worktops.

Cornice   Decorative timber moulding used to finish off the top of kitchen wall units.

Decor panel   Panel of the same material as the kitchen cabinet doors, used to hide the white door of a built-in appliance.

Domino hob   Modular hob put together to suit your needs and to fit into your worktop. Component options include electric, gas or ceramic rings, a deep fat fryer and a wok.

Epoxy grout   Waterproof and bacteria-resistant grout used mainly on tiled worktops.

Fillers   Narrow strips made of the material that faces the units.

Flatpack   Self-assembly kitchen units packed flat and in pieces for you to assemble yourself.

Free-standing Appliances that fit into a gap between units, leaving space on either side.

Fully integrated Built-in appliances in a unit with doors to match the rest of the kitchen.

Inset sinks see Self-rimming bowls

Integral sinks Sinks made of the same material as the worktop (see Corian).

Island unit Free-standing work station in the middle of the kitchen.

Kickspace The recessed plinth between the bottom shelf of base units and the floor.

Kickspace heater Fan-assisted convector heater fitted into the kickspace.

Laminated worktop Chipboard with a plastic laminate surface, often with a rounded-off post-formed front edge.

Liming Technique whereby white lime is rubbed into the grain of oak to make it more noticeable.

Modular Kitchen fitted out with a range of standard-sized units and accessories.

Monobloc tap Mixer tap with a single spout, mounted over a single pipe supply hole at the edge of the sink.

Multifunctional oven Multi-purpose oven with settings that include conventional, fan-assisted, steam and rotisserie options.

Peninsula unit Base units and worktop which extends across the room.

Plinth Panel which fits between the floor and the bottom of the base units and hides the unit's adjustable legs from view.

Post-formed worktop Laminated worktop with a rounded-off front edge.

Range Large cooker, normally with two ovens and several hob plates, powered by electric, gas or solid fuel.

Self-rimming bowls Sink bowls with a rounded edge that fits over the worktop; also known as inset sinks.

Slot-in Free-standing appliances which can slide in between fitted units.

Splashback Area behind the sink or hob which has been treated to protect the walls from splashes.

Undermounted sink Sink mounted under the worktop, so the work surface overhangs the edge of the sink bowl.

picture credits

All photographs of Anne McKevitt's designs by **Colin Poole**. © 1997 and 1998 **Colin Poole**
Photography Art Direction and Styling by **Anne McKevitt**

The publisher wishes to thank the photographers and organizations for their kind permission to reproduce the following photographs in this book:

2-3 Camera Press; 4-5 Anita Calereo/*House & Garden*/Hatch House; 6 *Vogue Living*; 7 above The Interior Archive/Henry Wilson; 7 below *Marie Claire Maison*/Francis Amiand/Christine Puech; 8 left Verne; 8 right Vitsoe 0171 354 8444; 9 *Belle*; 10 Undine Prohl; 11 left *Belle*; 11 right *Marie Claire Maison*/Marie-Pierre Morel/Marie Kalt; 14-15 Ray Main; 30 left Tim Street-Porter/designer Brian Murphy; 30 right *Marie Claire Maison*/Marie Pierre Morel/Marie Kalt; 31 *Belle*; 38 below Tim Street-Porter/Architect Brian Murphy; 42 Nadia Mackenzie; 43 above Ray Main/Architect Susanna Lumsden; 43 below Arcaid/Nicholas Kane/Architect Gary Webb; 44 Camera Press; 48 left *Vogue Living*/Darren Centofanti; 48 right Dia Press; 49 *Eigenhuis*/Paul Wiering; 56 left Arcaid/*Belle*/Earl Carter/Architect Shane Chandler; 56 right Ray Main/Chris Cowper Architects; 57 Arcaid/*Belle*/Trevor Mein/Architect John Wardle; 64 above *Belle*; 64 below *House & Garden*, Australia; 65 above *Marie Claire Maison*/Gilles de Chabaneix/Catherine Ardouin; 65 below *Marie Claire Maison*/Marie Pierre Morel/Marie Kalt; 66 Ray Main; 76 *Marie Claire Maison*/Gilles de Chabaneix/Daniel Rozensztroch; 77 below Paul Ryan/designer Felix Bonnier; 77 above *Belle*; 82 Arcaid/Nicholas Kane/Ash Sakula Architects; 83 above *Belle*; 83 below Paul Ryan/Architects Hariri & Hariri; 84 *Marie Claire Maison*/Eric Morin/Catherine Ardouin; 85-87 above *Marie Claire Maison*/Eric Morin/Catherine Ardouin; 88 above *Marie Claire Maison*/Marie Pierre Morel/Marie Kalt; 88 below Paul Ryan/designer Gordon & De Vries; 89 Ray Main/Architect Chris Cowper; 90 Ray Main/Leeds Loft Company; 96 left Paul Ryan/Architect David Ling; 97 left *Marie Claire Maison*/Ingalill Snitt/Catherine Ardouin; 96 right *Marie Claire Maison*/Gilles de Chabaneix/Catherine Ardouin; 97 right *Vogue Living*; 104 left *Marie Claire Maison*/Nicolas Tosi/Catherine Ardouin; 104 right *Marie Claire Maison*/Nicolas Tosi/Catherine Ardouin; 105 Nadia Mackenzie/Paula Pryke; 110 left *Vogue Living*/photographer Simon Kenny; 110 right Arcaid/Nicholas Kane/designed by Ash Sakula Architects; 111 left Anita Calero/*House & Garden*/Hatch House; 111 right *Marie Claire Maison*/Francis Amiand/Julie Borgeaud; 116 The Interior Archive/Fritz von Schulenburg; 124 left *Marie Claire Maison*/Marie Pierre Morel/Postic; 124 right Robert Harding Picture Library/Jan Baldwin/*Homes & Gardens*/© IPC Magazines; 125 Ray Main/Granit Architects; 126–127 *VT Wonen*/Dennis Brandsma; 128 above Noble Russell Furniture 01572 821591/designer Laurence Noble/photographer Stephen Henderson; 128 below *Marie Claire Maison*/Gilles de Chabaneix; 129 above *Belle*; 129 below Arcaid/*Belle*/Simon Kenny/designer Helen Quinn; 138 above *Marie Claire Maison*/Marie Pierre Morel; 138 below *VT Wonen*/Dennis Brandsma; 139 Arcaid/*Belle*/Trevor Mein/Architect John Wardle; 157 above left *VT Wonen*/Dennis Brandsma; 157 centre right *VT Wonen*/Dennis Brandsma.

acknowledgements

Extra special thanks to:

Don for being superhuman.

Colin Poole for his talent and never flinching at my 36-hour working days and smiling throughout it all.

Annabelle Poole, now known as Mrs Polaroid, for being fantastic and stepping in as my part-time stylist when my mobile rang.

Pauline Savage for being the smiliest, sweetest slave-driver on the planet.

Baggy and **Sooty**, my two cats, for overseeing all photo shoots, walking across my text and sleeping across spreads that I needed to check urgently. I couldn't have written House Sensation without them. Really.

Anthea Morton-Saner for always believing, being a tough nut and a softy on the inside.

Anne Furniss for believing in the book.

Mary Evans for turning my layout ideas on scraps of paper into reality.

Simon Balley and **Joanna Hill** for working so hard to make the design happen.

Martin Butler, John Duckworth, Wesley Bolton, Frank Farci, Keith Fuller and **Robin Spilsbury** for turning my terrible drawings into fantastic real designs.

Everyone at the **BBC Home Front office** for making my life frantic.

Samira Higham for her guidance, direction and terrible mimicry of a Scottish accent.

Neill Bristow, model maker extraordinaire. If I'd know you were this good I'd never have bothered doing life-sized rooms.

With thanks to:

The **BBC** for use of its copyright material and projects featured on pages 5, 13, 22–29, 32–39, 50–55, 58–63, 68–75, 98–103, 108–109, 112–115, 132–137, 149–152, 155–160, 162–173, 176–181, 183.

Into their homes:

Melanie Cantor, Neil & Diane Williams, Alison Reynolds, Hermoine Camron, Sacha Wescourt, Tina Bolton, Jim & Catriona McQueen, Nicky & Peter Williamson, Glyn & Katrina Isherwood, Emma Fischel & John Sleeman, Diane Arthur, Brian & Emma Wares, Richard, Matt & Ben.

Also thanks to:

Steve Anderson, Kaye Godleman, Elaine Navickas, Daisy Goodwin, Simon Shaw, Franny Moyle, Linda Stephens, Owen Gaye, Kim Evans, Mary Sackville-West, Nicky Grant.

Nicola Pointer, Heidi Perry, Amelia Dare, Marielle Wyse, Lindi Doye, Angela Holden, Maggi Gibson, Janine Josman, James Strong, Philippa Ransford, Troy, Nick Watson.

Sarah Clarke, Ellis Jamieson, Dennie Pasion, John Dutton, Barry Preedy, Helen Beney, Sam Ruston, William Martin, Camron PR, Michael Kamlish, Jo Thiel, Colin Mitchell-Rose, Sarah McAvoy, Greg Demosthenous, Scott Phillips.

Thanks to the following organizations and individuals for supplies and services:

pages 16–21 The Conran Shop; Dulux; The Easy Chair Co.; John Egan & Sons; Freemans; Habitat; Hitch Mylius; Ikea; Jacobs, Young & Westbury; Mulberry Home; Nu Line Builders; Optelma Lighting; Preedy Glass; Arthur Sanderson & Sons; Thames & Hudson (*Tribes* by Art Wolfe); WLB Carpentry (from designs by Anne McKevitt).

pages 22–23 Dulux; Jali Ltd (from a design by Anne McKevitt); Neal Street East; The Stencil Library.

pages 24–29 Angelic; Biz; Dulux; The Holding Co.; Ikea; John Lewis; Nu Line; Pearson's Cycles; Russell & Chapple; Unidec Distributors; Wickes.

pages 32–37 African Escape; B & Q; Chelsea Gardener; The Conran Shop; Dulux; Extraordinary Designs; Freemans; Keith Fuller; Habitat; Ikea; Jali (from a design by Anne McKevitt); Olympic Blinds; Oxfam; Plasti-Kote; Romsey Reclamation; Suzanne Ruggles; Space.

pages 38–39 R K Alliston; BHS; Cargo Home Shop; The Conran Shop; Dulux; Fired Earth; Keith Fuller; The General Trading Co.; Nu Line Builders; Ocean; Plasterworks; The Platonic Fireplace Co.; Preedy Glass; Purves & Purves; World's End Tiles.

pages 40–41 Allied Carpets; Crayford Tubes; Dulux; Habitat; Ikea; Paperchase; Silent Gliss; John Wilman.

pages 46–47 Arthur Beale Ltd; Dulux; Formica; Gooding Aluminium; Ikea; MFI.

pages 50–55 Aktiva; Bliss; Deborah Services Ltd; Divertimenti; Dulux; William T Eden; Formica; Freudenberg Building Systems; Habitat;

Hafele; House of Fraser; Ikea; Jali Ltd (from a design by Anne McKevitt); John Lewis; Macroe Windows Ltd; Mosaic Workshop; Ocean; Paperchase; Purves & Purves; Tienda; Valli & Valli.

pages 58–63 Emma Bernhardt; John Duckworth (from a design by Anne McKevitt); Dulux; Formica; Freemans; The Holding Co.; Inflate; Jali Ltd; MGA Interserve Ltd; Joni Rokotnitz.

pages 68–75 Acco; Craig & Rose; Deralam; Dulux; Freemans; Habitat; Ikea; John Lewis; MFI; Mathmos; Nice Irmas; Helen Rawlinson; Sewing & Crafts Superstore; The Source; Townsends; Wallbeds Direct; Windsor & Newton; WLB Carpentry.

pages 78–81 Habitat; Ikea; Olympic Blinds; Paperchase; Stanfords.

pages 92–95 B & Q; Brausch & Co.; Descamps; Frank Farci; Habitat; Harvey Maria; Ideal Standard; Ikea; Jali Ltd (from a design by Anne McKevitt); Original Bathrooms; Preedy Glass; Thames & Hudson (*Tribes* by Art Wolfe); Villeroy & Boch; Wickes.

pages 98–103 The Conran Shop; Dulux; Hansgrohe (shower and body jets by Phillipe Stark); P C Henderson; Kayode Lipede; Keeling Heating Products; Marble Ideas; Mr Resistor; Myson Heat Exchange; Norcros Adhesives; Oakleaf Joinery; Paramount; Pilkington UK; Preedy Glass; Paula Pryke Flowers; Saint Gobain Solaglas; W & G Sissons; Robin Spilsbury; Stonell; Stuart Turner Ltd; Svedbergs; Time Design; Worcester Heat Systems.

pages 106–107 Dulux; Heals; Ikea; Mosaic Workshop; The Pier; Preedy Glass; Wickes.

pages 108–109 Bathing Beauties; Sarah Clarke; The Conran Shop; First Floor; John Lewis; Next; Stoney Parsons.

pages 112–113 Amari Plastics; Amtico; Aston Matthews; Bliss; Bobo Designs; Cargo; The Conran Shop; Dulux; Freemans; Homebase; Ikea; Preedy Glass; The Source; Variety Floors Group; X Film UK Ltd.

pages 118–123 Bollom & Co; Borovicks; Dorma; Keith Fuller; Habitat; Hitch Mylius; Ikea; Jali Ltd (from a design by Anne McKevitt); MFI; Mulberry Home; Optelma Lighting; Plasti-Kote; Arthur Sanderson & Sons Ltd; Valli & Valli; Wickes.

pages 130–131 Dulux; Habitat; Ikea; The Iron Bed Co.; Leyland Paints; Scumble Goosie; Silent Gliss; Soho Silks; John Wilman.

pages 132–137 Aktiva Systems; Armitage Shanks; Aston Matthews; B & Q; BHS; Bisque; Candell Lighting Ltd; Caradon Plumbing Solutions; Dulux; John Dutton & Partners; William T Eden Plc; Elite Tiles; Fired Earth; HAF; The Holding Co.; House of Fraser; Ikea; Muji; Novatec (blinds designed by Alison White); Oakleaf Joinery (carpenter Gerry Minton); Optelma Lighting; PIU Incandescent; Planet Organic; Ralph Lauren Home Collection; The Source; Stewart Turner Ltd; The Velux Company Ltd; Vola UK; West Ten Glass; Wicanders; Wickes.

stockists & suppliers

Acco UK Ltd
stationery manufacturers
Gatehouse Road
Aylesbury
Bucks HP19 3DT
tel: 0800 252359

African Escape
Tribal art
Brian & Susy Reeves
127 Portobello Road
London W11 2DY
tel: 0171 221 6650

Aktiva Systems Ltd
lighting designers &
manufacturers
10b Spring Place
Kentish Town
London NW5 3BH
tel: 0171 722 9439

Allied Carpets
carpet suppliers
tel: 0181 507 7240 for branches

R K Alliston
gardening designers & retailers
183 New Kings Road
London SW6 4SW
tel: 0171 731 8100

Amari Plastics
stockists & distributors
tel: 01932 835000 for branches

Amtico
flooring suppliers
CMT Ltd
Kingfield Road
Coventry CV6 5PL
tel: 01203 861500

Angelic Candles Ltd
candle suppliers
Highgate Business Centre
Greenwood Place
London NW5 1LB
tel: 0171 221 3414

Armitage Shanks
bathroom fittings suppliers
tel: 01543 490253 for stockists

Artisan
curtain rail retailers
4a Union Court
20 Union Road
London SW4 6JP
tel: 0171 498 6974

Aston Matthews
bathroom retailers
141–147 Essex Road
London N1 2SN
tel: 0171 226 3657

Bathing Beauties
classic bathrooms
manufacturers & retailers
43 Muswell Hill Road
London N10 3JB
tel: 0181 365 2794

Arthur Beale Ltd
yacht chandlers
194 Shaftesbury Avenue
London WC2H 8JP
tel: 0171 836 9034

Emma Bernhardt
accessories suppliers
301 Portobello Road
London W10 5TE
tel: 0181 960 2929

BHS Plc
department store
tel: 0171 262 3288 for branches

Bobo Designs
interiors & furniture designers
10 Southampton Street
Brighton BN2 2UT
tel: 01273 684753

Bisque
radiator suppliers
244 Belsize Road
London NW6 4BT
tel: 0171 328 2225

Biz Ltd
zinc & stainless steel
fabricators
Millmarsh Lane
Brinsdown
Middlesex EN3 2QA
tel: 0181 443 3300

Bliss Ltd
clocks, kitchen/bathroom
products
Paradise Works
Arden Forest Estate
Alcester
Warwickshire B49 6EH
tel: 01789 400077

Bollom & Co. Ltd
paint manufacturers
PO Box 78
Croydon Road
Beckenham
Kent BR3 4BL
tel: 0181 658 2299

Borovick's Fabrics Ltd
fabric suppliers
16 Berwick Street
London W1V 4HP
tel: 0171 437 2180

B & Q Plc
DIY Supercentre
tel: 01703 256 256 for branches

Brausch & Co.
bathroom distributors
The Gate Centre
Great West Road
Brentford TW8 9DD
tel: 0181 847 4455

The Building Centre
industry information
26 Store Street
London WC1E 7BT
tel: 0171 637 1022

Candell Lighting Ltd
lighting suppliers
20–22 Avenue Mews
Muswell Hill
London N10 3NP
tel: 0181 444 9004

**Caradon Plumbing
Solutions**
plumbing manufacturers
Cromwell Road
Cheltenham
Gloucs GL52 5EP
tel: 01242 221 221

Cargo Home Shops
homeware retailers
209 Tottenham Court Road
London W1P 9AF
tel: 0171 580 2895

Chelsea Gardener Ltd
garden centre
125 Sydney Street
London SW3 6NR
tel: 0171 352 5656

Sarah Clarke
seamstress
tel: 0181 672 7189

The Conran Shop
home furnishing retailers
Michelin House
81 Fulham Road
London SW3 6RD
tel: 0171 589 7401

Craig & Rose Plc
varnish & paint suppliers
tel: 0131 554 1131 for stockists

Crayford Tubes
cardboard tube manufacturers
Unit 33 Acorn Industrial Park
Crayford
Kent BA1 4AL
tel: 01322 526614

Deborah Services Ltd
contract scaffolders
731–761 Harrow Road
London NW10 5NY
tel: 0181 969 3676

Deralam Laminates Ltd
laminate suppliers
Unit 462–464
Ranglet
Preston PR5 8AR
tel: 01772 315 888

Descamps
bedlinen & towelling suppliers
197 Sloane Street
London SW1X NQX
tel: 0171 235 6957

Divertimenti
specialist houseware suppliers
Ericol House
93–99 Upper Richmond Road
London SW15 2TG
tel: 0181 246 4300

Dorma
bedding specialists
PO Box 7 Lees Street
Swinton
Manchester M27 6DB
tel: 0161 251 4400

Dulux
paint suppliers
tel: 01753 550 555 for information

**John Dutton &
Partners builders**
14 The Grove
London W5 5LH
tel: 0181 840 2050

stockists & suppliers

The Easy Chair Co.
upholstery suppliers
30 Lyndhurst Road
Worthing
Sussex BN11 2DF
tel: 01903 201081

William T Eden Plc
wood panel products suppliers
Crown Wharf
Whitewall Way
Finsbury
Rochester
Kent ME2 4EP
tel: 01634 291212

John Egan & Sons
sundries
339 Flower Market
New Covent Garden Market
London SW8 5NH
tel: 0171 720 4147

Elite Tiles
specialist tiles suppliers
Elite House
The Broadway
London NW9 7BP
tel: 0181 202 1806

Extraordinary Designs
lighting designers
3b Kings Street Mews
Kings Street
London N2 8DY
tel: 0181 883 3887

Frank Farci
carpenter
tel: 0181 459 2507/0956 371304

Fired Earth
tiles, carpets, paints, rugs
tel: 01295 812088 for branches

First Floor
flooring suppliers
174 Wandsworth Bridge Road
London SW6 2VQ
tel: 0171 736 1123

Formica
laminate manufacturers
Coast Road
North Shields
Tyne & Wear NE29 8RE
tel: 0191 259 3000

Freemans Plc
home furnishing & clothing retailers
tel: 0800 900200 for information

**Freudenberg
Building Systems**
hardware suppliers
Gilmorton Road
Lutteworth
Leicestershire LE17 4DU
tel: 01455 553081

Keith Fuller
builders & decorators, fireplaces
tel: 0181 330 0620/0802 346282

The General Trading Co.
general suppliers
144 Sloane Street
London SW1X 9BL
tel: 0171 730 0411

Gooding Aluminium
aluminium suppliers
& fabricators
1 British Wharf
Landmannway
London SE14 5RS
tel: 0181 692 2255

Habitat
home furnishing retailers
tel: 0645 334433 for branches

HAF
iron mongery manufacturers
Haf House Mead Lane
Hertford
Herts SG13 7AP
tel: 01992 505655

Hafele
kitchen & furniture
fittings suppliers
tel: 0181 551 8888 for information

Hansgrohe
homeware retailers
Sandown Trading Estate
Royal Mills
Surrey KT10 8BL
tel: 01372 465655

Harvey Maria Ltd
tile designers (mail order only)
tel: 0171 350 1964

Heals
home furnishing retailers
tel: 0171 631 1666 for branches

P C Henderson
garage manufacturers
Durham Road
Durham DH6 5NG
tel: 0191 377 0701

Hitch Mylius
furniture suppliers
Alma House
301 Alma Road
Middlesex EN3 7BB
tel: 0181 443 2616

The Holding Co.
storage product retailers
241–245 Kings Road
London SW3 5EL
tel: 0171 352 1600

Homebase
DIY Supercentre
tel: 0181 784 7200 for branches

Homeworks
furniture retailers
tel: 0800 192192 for information

House of Fraser
department store
tel: 0171 963 2000 for branches

Ideal Standard Ltd
bathroom suppliers
The Bathroom Works
National Avenue
Hull HU5 4HS
tel: 01482 346461

Ikea
home furnishing retailers
tel: 0181 208 5600 for branches

Inflate
PVC products retailers
5 Old Street
London EC1V 9HL
tel: 0171 251 5453

The Iron Bed Co.
iron bed retailers
384 Fulham Road
London SW6 5NT
tel: 0171 610 9903

Jacobs, Young & Westbury
furniture suppliers
Bridge Road
Haywards Heath
West Sussex RH16 1UA
tel: 01444 412411

Jali Ltd
fretwork suppliers
Apsley House
Chartham
Canterbury
Kent CT4 7HT
tel: 01227 831710

John Lewis
department store
tel: 0171 629 7711 for branches

Kayode Lipede
concrete designers
6 Iroko House
Lightos Road
London NW3 6ER
tel: 0171 794 7535

Keeling Heating Products
heated towel rail
manufacturers
Units 1–2
Dock Road
Gosport
Hampshire PO12 1SJ
tel: 01705 796633

Lakeland Ltd
homeware distributors
tel: 01539 488100 (mail order)

Lassco Flooring
flooring specialists
101–108 Britannia Walk
London N1 7LU
tel: 0171 252 5157

Leyland SDM
specialist decorators
merchants
tel: 0800 454 484 for stockists

Macroe Windows Ltd
window manufacturers
& retailers
Units OPQ
Cradock Road
Luton LU4 0JF
tel: 01582 585867

Marble Ideas Ltd
marble & granite suppliers
58 Wallingford Road
Uxbrisge Trading Estate
Uxbridge UB8 2RW
tel: 01895 254500

Mathmos Direct
decorative lighting
179 Drury Lane
Covent Garden
London WC2B 5QF
tel: 0171 405 6990

MFI
furniture stores
tel: 0800 192192 for branches

stockists & suppliers

MGA Interserve Ltd
kitchen components
manufacturers
Unit 17
Capcote Trading Estate
Powke Lane
Cradeley Heath
B64 5QR
tel: 01384 638700

Mosaic Workshop
made to order mosaic pieces
Unit B
443–449 Holloway Road
London N7 6LJ
tel: 0171 263 2997

Mr Resistor
electrical wholesalers
& retailers
82–84 New Kings Road
Fulham SW6 FLU
tel: 0171 736 7521

Muji
homewares &
clothing retailers
26 Great Marlborough Street
London W1 1HO
tel: 0171 584 1197

Mulberry Home
homeware retailers
Mulberry Co. Ltd
Shepton Mallet
Bath BA4 5NF
tel: 01749 340593

Myson Heat Exchange
heating manufacturers
1515 Hedon Road
Hull
North Humberside HU9 5NX
tel: 0345 697509

Neal Street East
oriental specialists
5 Neal Street
Covent Garden
London WC2H 9PU
tel: 0171 240 0135

Next
home furnishings & clothing
tel: 0345 100500 for information

Nice Irmas by Post
home ideas
tel: 0181 343 7610 (mail order)

Norcros Adhesives
adhesive suppliers
Longton Road
Trentham
Stoke-on-Trent ST4 8JB
tel: 01782 591100

Norema Interiors Ltd
rigid Scandinavian kitchens
3 Middle Pavement
Nottingham
Notts NG1 7DX
tel: 0115 947 3177

Novatec
blinds manufacturers & retailers
Star Lane
Margate
Kent CT9 4EF
tel: 01843 604430

Nu Line Builders Merchants
building materials suppliers
315 Westbourne Park Road
London W11 1EF
tel: 0171 727 7748

Nutshell Natural Paints
paint retailer
Hamlyn House
Mardle Way
Buckfastleigh
Devon TQ11 0NR
tel: 01733 211 355

Oakleaf Joinery
staircase commissions,
woodturning specialists
Unit 5
Nene Terrace
Crowlands
Lincs PE6 0LD
tel: 01733 211 355

Ocean Home Shopping
home furnishings suppliers
tel: 0800 132985 (mail order)

Olympic Blinds
blinds manufacturers & retailers
14 Cosgrove Way
Luton LU1 1XL
tel: 01582 738878

Optelma Lighting UK Ltd
lighting manufacturers &
distributors
14 Napier Court
Abingdon
Oxon OX14 3NB
tel: 01235 553769

Original Bathrooms
bathroom furnishings suppliers
143–145 Kew Road
Richmond-upon-Thames
Surrey TW9 2PN
tel: 0181 940 7554

Oxfam
ethnic artefacts & clothing retailers
tel: 01865 313 600 for branches

Paperchase
stationery & accessories suppliers
213 Tottenham Court Road
London W1P 9AF
tel: 0171 580 8496

Paramount Industries
stainless steel homewares
manufacturers
246 Kilburn Lane
London W10 4BA
tel: 0181 960 0666

Stoney Parsons
stained glass designer
(works to commission)
3 The Courtyard
41 Ezra Street
London E2 7RH
tel/fax: 0171 729 6389

Pearson's Cycles –
cycles & accessories suppliers
126 High Street
Sutton SM1 1LU
tel: 0181 642 2095

The Pier
homeware retailers
tel: 0171 814 5020 for branches

Pilkington UK Ltd
glass and window manufacturers
Prescot Road
St Helens
Merseyside WA10 3TT
tel: 01744 28882

Plasterworks
plaster manufacturers & retailers
38 Cross Street
London N1 2BG
tel: 0171 226 5355

Plasti-Kote Ltd
aerosol paint manufacturers
(available at most DIY stores)
London Road Industrial Estate
Sawston
Cambridge CB2 4TR
tel: 01223 836400

The Platonic Fireplace Co.
modern firegrate & geolog
manufacturers
40 Peterborough Road
London SW6 3BN
tel: 0171 610 9440

Preedy Glass
glass manufacturers & retailers
Lamb Works
North Road
London N7 9DP
tel: 0171 700 0377

Paula Pryke Flowers
flower sellers
20 Penton Street
London N1
tel: 0171 837 7336

Purves & Purves
contemporary furnishings
specialists
80, 81 & 83 Tottenham Court
Road
London W1
tel: 0171 580 8223

**Ralph Lauren Home
Collection**
home furnishings collection
tel: 0171 235 5010 for stockists

Helen Rawlinson
textile & object designer
The Chocolate Factory
Unit 5, First Floor
Farleigh Place
London N16 7SX
tel: 0171 503 5839

RenuBath Ltd
bath renovators
76–78 Cricklade Street
Cirencester
Gloucs GL7 1JN
tel: 01285 656624

Joni Rokotnitz
murals & graphics painter
tel: 0171 252 6769/0171 738 7878

Romsey Reclamation
reclaimed building
& roofing merchants
Station Approach
Romsey Railway Station
Hampshire SO51 8DU
tel: 01794 524174

stockists & suppliers

Suzanne Ruggles
furniture designer & retailer
436 Kings Road
London SW10 0LJ
tel: 0171 351 6565

Russell & Chapple
art suppliers
23 Monmouth Street
London WC2H 9DE
tel: 0171 836 7521

Saint-Gobain Solaglas
glass retailers
Herald Way
Binley
Coventry CV3 2ND
tel: 01203 458 844
Internet: www.glassfacts.co.uk

Arthur Sanderson & Sons Ltd
fabric retailers
112–120 Brompton Road
London SW3 1JJ
tel: 0171 584 3344

Scumble Goosie Ltd
ready-to-paint furniture
& accessories
Lewiston Mill
Toadsmoor Road
Stroud
Gloucestershire GL5 2TB
tel: 01453 731305
Internet: www.scumble-goosie.co.uk

Sewing & Crafts Superstore
crafts supplies
300 Balham High Street
London SW17 7AA
tel: 0181 767 0036

Silent Gliss Ltd
curtain tracks & blinds
manufacturers
tel: 0171 288 6100 for stockists

W & G Sissons
stainless steel, sanitary ware &
catering equipment manufacturers
Carrwood Road
Sheepbridge
Chesterfield S41 9QB
tel: 01246 450255

Sofa Workshop Direct
sofa manufacturers
tel: 01443 238699 (mail order)

Soho Silks
fabric retailers & wholesalers
24 Berwick Street
London W1V 3RS
tel: 0171 434 3305

The Source
homeware retailers
26–40 Kensington High Street
London W8 4PF
tel: 0171 937 2626

Space
homeware retailers
214 Westbourne Grove
London W11 2RH
tel: 0171 229 6533

Robin Spilsbury Designs
interior construction
18 Great Pulteney Street
Bath BA2 4BR
tel: 01225 461451

Stanfords Maps
maps & travel booksellers
12–14 Long Acre
Covent Garden
London WC2E 9LP
tel: 0171 836 1321

The Stencil Library
stencil retailers
tel: 01661 844844 (mail order)

Stonell Ltd
floor & wall tiles suppliers
Forstal House
Beltring
Paddock Wood
Kent TN12 6PY
tel: 01892 833500

Svedbergs
bathroom products
17 Fulham Road
London SW6 5UL
tel: 0171 371 9214

Tienda
shopfitters
Occupation Road
South Witham
Grantham
Lincs NG33 5PZ
tel: 01572 767111

Time Design
neon lighting designers
54 Gloucester Mews
London W2 3HE
tel: 0171 262 0717

Townsends
antique & reproduction
fireplace manufacturers
18 Abbey Road
London NW8 0AE
tel: 0171 624 4756

Trent Bathrooms
bathroom sanitary ware
PO Box 290
Hanley
Stoke-on-Trent
Staffs ST1 3RR
tel: 01782 202334

Stewart Turner Ltd
water pumps manufacturers
& retailers
47 Market Place
Henley on Thames
Oxon RG9 2AD
tel: 01491 572655

Valli & Valli Ltd
furniture fitters
8 Gerard
Lichfield Industrial Estate
Tamworth
Staffordshire B79 7UW
tel: 01827 63352

Variety Floors Ltd
floor & wall finish contractors
263 Cowley Road
Oxford OX4 1YE
tel: 01865 249044

The Velux Co. Ltd
roof windows & accessories
manufacturers & retailers
Woodside Way
Fife KY7 4ND
Scotland
tel: 01592 772211

Villeroy & Boch
bathroom manufacturers
& distributors
267 Merton Road
London SW18 5JS
tel: 0181 871 4028

Vola UK Ltd
glass basin & taps distributors
Unit 12, Ampthill Business Park
Station Road
Ampthill
Beds MK45 2QW
tel: 01525 841155

Wallbeds Direct
wallbeds manufacturer
Linen House
162–168 Regent Street
London W2 3HE
tel: 0171 434 2066

West Ten Glass Ltd
glass manufacturers & retailers
485 Latimer Road
North Kensington
London W10 6RD
tel: 0181 969 5682

Wicanders
wooden flooring manufacturers
& distributors
Amorim House
Star Road
Horsham
West Sussex RH13 8RA
tel: 01403 710001

Wickes
DIY superstore
tel: 0800 300 328 for branches

John Wilman
fabric suppliers
tel: 0800 581984 for information

Windsor & Newton
art suppliers
tel: 0181 427 4343 for stockists

WLB Carpentry
wood specialists
Flat 2
66 Sutherland Avenue
London W9 2QS
tel: 0956 502067

Worcester Heat Systems
boiler and central heating
system manufacturers
tel: 01905 754624 for information

World's End Tiles
tile manufacturers & distributors
Silver Thorne Road
London SW8 3HE
tel: 0171 819 2100

X Film UK Ltd
self-adhesive vinyl retailers
tel: 0800 453308 for information

index

index